D0986836

Learning Centers...

A Guide for Effective Use

Louise F. Waynant
Howard County, Maryland
Board of Education

Robert M. Wilson
University of Maryland

The Instructo Corporation
A Subsidiary of McGraw-Hill
Paoli, Pennsylvania 19301

Editorial Direction: *Roberta Richards*
Editorial Assistants: *Lea S. Bramnick, Hugh Douglass,*
H. Ronald Hodgins, Paula Librett
Cecilia Powers Wright, Dianne Yeager
Cover Design: *Gilbert Lieberman*
Illustrations: *Donald W. Patterson*
Art Assistants: *Sära Rasmussen, Jane Smyth, Angela Tocci*

The authors wish to thank the following people for their input to this book:

Marcia Barnes   *Kitty McGrogan*
Gail Brotman   *Linda Miller*
Joseph Czarnecki   *Larry Nash*
Ellen Hormanski   *Jeri Ribovich*

Robert Wilson.

Current printing (last digit):

10   9   8   7   6   5

Library of Congress Cataloging in Publication Data

Waynant, Louise F
   Learning centers.

   Bibliography: p.
   1. Activity programs in education. I. Wilson, Robert Mills, joint author. II. Title.
LB1027.W37   371.3'078   74-3463
ISBN 0-07-082044-9

Table of Contents

How to Use This Book
. . . A Learning Center

PURPOSE OF THE CENTER:

The purpose of this learning center is to guide readers in using the book to assist them with planning, developing, maintaining, and evaluating learning centers.

ACTIVITIES:

I: Identify Your Questions about Learning Centers (Turn to page v for directions)

II: Locate Answers to Your Questions (Turn to page v for directions)

III: Add More Ideas to the Idea Bank After You've Tried Some of the Ideas Presented in This Book

ACTIVITY I:
IDENTIFY YOUR QUESTIONS ABOUT LEARNING CENTERS

Directions

1. Think about the questions you have concerning learning centers.

2. Read each question listed on the QUESTION IDENTIFICATION CHART on page vi. (These were the questions which were asked most frequently by more than 300 educators who responded to a survey in which they listed three major questions they had about learning centers.)

3. Place a check in Column A (Have Information) if the question is one to which you already have a satisfactory answer.

4. Place a check in Column B (Need Information) if the question is one which you would like to have answered.

5. List additional questions you would like to have answered in the blanks provided.

ACTIVITY II:
LOCATE ANSWERS TO YOUR QUESTIONS

Directions

1. For answers to questions Number 1 - Number 13, refer to the chapters indicated on the **Question Identification Chart.** Refer to the **Index** and to the **Annotated Bibliography** in order to obtain answers to additional questions you have listed.

2. As answers to your questions are obtained, check the appropriate boxes in Column A.

ACTIVITY III:
ADD IDEAS TO THE IDEA BANK

Directions

1. Use centers in your classroom!

2. Add ideas you try, and ideas you obtain from colleagues, workshops, and conferences to the **Idea Bank** in the back of this handbook.

G O O D   L U C K !

QUESTION IDENTIFICATION CHART

Check the appropriate boxes according to the directions presented in Activity I and Activity II on page v.

Question	A Have Information	B Need Information	C Reference Refer to Chapter
General			
1. What are learning centers and what are their characteristics?	|||	|||	1, 2
2. Why should I use learning centers in my classroom?			1
3. How can I get started with centers?			2, 4
Construction			
4. How do I make a center?	|||	|||	2
5. How can I save time in the construction of centers?			2
Management			
6. How do I organize my classroom for centers?	|||	|||	3
7. When should I use centers?			3
8. How can I help students work independently?			1, 3, 4
Ideas			
9. Where can I obtain more ideas on centers?					7
Evaluation			
10. How do I evaluate student progress with centers?	|||	|||	5
11. How do I evaluate my centers?			5
12. How can I meet the needs of all my students?			1, 2
Problems			
13. What problems have teachers had in using centers?	|||	|||	6
14. _____?			Refer to
15. _____?			Index and
16. _____?			Annotated
17. _____?			Bibliography

Chapter 1

Introduction to Learning Centers

hat are learning centers and what are their characteristics?
ny should I use learning centers with my students?
ow can I meet the needs of all my students?

There is no one definition of a learning center. In this book we will
e referring to learning centers as a means of organizing instruction so
nat students can direct much of their own learning. In fact, we will
e contending that any learning, reinforcement, or interest activity
n which a student can direct his own learning is a learning center.

One of the major objectives of all instruction is to assist the stu-
ent to become a self-directing learner. All teachers want students to
e able to know how to choose objectives, to select materials to meet
hose objectives, and to evaluate their own learning. Students learn to
ecome self-directing when they are given alternatives from which to
hoose. Learning centers are one effective way for teachers to develop
ctivities so that students can make their own choices.

Why self-directing? The obvious answer is that for learning to continue beyond a student's relationship with his teachers, he must learn to make reasonable choices, see his own way toward solutions to those choices, and be self-fulfilled.

Why learning centers? All teachers need to supply students with many learning activities. The trend toward individualization of instruction calls for activities designed to meet the strengths and needs of every student. Learning centers can do just that. But, perhaps more important, learning centers can lead students toward commitment to their learning. Since centers provide stimulating activities, choice, and decision-making opportunities, the use of learning centers is an unusually effective instructional technique. In addition, teachers and students have found that learning centers can make learning more enjoyable. So read on and see if learning centers can become a part of your curriculum.

Characteristics of Learning Centers

As stated before, learning centers have one major characteristic - that of self-direction. Any activity in which students direct their own learning may well be considered a learning center. To be self-directing, the activity must allow for the student to move through the activity successfully without teacher direction. Among the specific characteristics of learning activities which foster self-direction are:

1. Clear directions: Directions help a student to proceed through an activity in the necessary manner without consultation with the teacher.

2. Clearly stated objectives: When students know why they are working with an activity, their efforts are more purposeful and better organized. They also become better able to determine when they have reached the objective of the center activity.

3. Choice: When you provide students with activities that allow them to make choices, you facilitate individualization. It should not make any difference which activity they choose as long as the objective is met.

4. Multi-level activities: Since all students start from different points, it is important to provide activities which begin at different levels. Multi-level centers contain activities which vary in difficulty. This makes the centers appropriate for many students. By making centers multi-

level, each student can enter at that point where he can be most successful, and work with as many challenging activities as he can.

5. Answers: When answers are readily available, the student does not need to rely upon the teacher to "correct" his work. It is especially important in learning situations where specific answers are involved to have those answers close at hand.

6. Manipulative as well as paper and pencil activities: Self-direction is enhanced when students can decide whether to work with pencil and paper or to work with activities which allow for more manipulative expression.

7. Opportunities to work in small groups: When students work in pairs or small groups, opportunities for self-direction are increased. Students learn together readily and find reassurance in being able to assist other students. Such team work leads to self-direction when one student begins to understand how another deals with a given assignment.

There is no need to provide for all of these characteristics in every learning activity to make it a learning center. In fact, it is often impossible to do so. Instead, consider the possibility of including these characteristics in activities which you develop. The more of them you include, the better the chances are that you will lead students toward self-direction. As one remembers that self-direction is what learning centers are all about, one will continue to make them with more and more of the characteristics which enhance self-direction.

As you read other literature on learning centers, you will find points of view different from those presented here. Some educators say a learning center is a special classroom for learning activities. Others say it is a place in the room where special activities are set up. However, when using this book, you should recall that learning centers include ALL of those activities which help students become self-directing in their own learning.

Meeting Individual Needs through Learning Centers

As students become free in their learning . . . that is, free from your constant supervision, you are also free. You can use your freedom to work with any student who needs your individual attention. This freedom is one effective way in which learning centers can help you meet individual needs of students.

By developing centers which are multi-level, you are moving a long way toward individualization of instruction. Instead of having every student in a given reading group do the same workbook page, you can now have a skill activity with as many levels as you want, creating the situation in which every student can be successful.

By providing students with opportunities to make choices, you are facilitating individualization of instruction. If you have an objective which can be met through learning centers which call either for written or oral responses, you can provide both options and let the students make the decision about which they prefer. Students will tend to choose those learning styles in which they are most comfortable and most successful.

Finally, you can provide for individualization by letting students help you construct learning centers. Your students will be certain to urge you to include activities and learning situations that are interesting and important to them. Each time you respond to these types of student suggestions - you are individualizing instruction.

Chapter 2

Developing Centers

How do I construct a learning center?
How can I save time in developing centers?

Developing learning centers can be a challenging, exciting project! Equipped with a set of objectives, a collection of materials, and a "blueprint" for construction, you can proceed effectively and efficiently. The suggestions which follow are offered as practical guidelines to help you develop centers. Most of these suggestions have come from classroom teachers who have used centers extensively.

What Is My Purpose, or Reason, for Developing the Center?

The essential first step in developing a center is to decide what the purpose of the center will be. Centers can serve several general purposes. You may decide that the purpose of the center will be to introduce new learning. Or, you may choose to have the center reinforce previous learning. A third alternative would be to have the center stimulate or extend interests. Still another general purpose would be to obtain diagnostic information concerning student progress with specific skills. Centers may be developed effectively for any one of these purposes, or for a combination of these purposes.

The purpose for which you plan your center may be one which reflects what you currently are teaching in any aspect of the school curriculum. Or, the purpose may be derived from a need for specific instruction which you have identified through diagnostic teaching. The purpose for which you plan the center also may relate to things such as current news events, popular holidays, or specific interests of students with whom you work.

The purpose for a center may be accomplished by combining content from several disciplines. For example, a center dealing with ecology may include math skills, science skills, social studies skills, and language arts skills. Such a multi-disciplined center provides an opportunity for students to integrate in a realistic way skills learned in separate content areas.

Here are some examples of purposes for center development:

1. Teacher A wanted her students to extend their word attack skills. She decided to develop a center to introduce the prefixes "anti" and "pro."

2. Teacher B had been working with comprehension skills in his classroom through focusing on the skill of identifying main ideas. He decided to develop a center to reinforce his students' abilities to identify main ideas.

3. Teacher C wished to extend the interest of his students in art as an expressive medium. He planned a center in which students described their reactions to poetry through art media.

4. Teacher D wished to gather diagnostic information concerning her students' ability to work with fractions. She planned a center containing some activities requiring very simple computations with fractions and other activities requiring more difficult computations with fractions.

What Specific Objectives Do I Wish Students to Meet through Using the Center?

After you have established a purpose for developing the center, you should make this decision: are there specific objectives which you want students to meet when they are using the center, or do you wish to have the center simply focus on the general purpose which you have identified? If you decide to identify specific objectives, it is helpful to list them in behavioral terms. Identifying and listing specific objectives for your center are particularly helpful in planning activities for the center and in evaluating student performance with the center activities.

Some examples of specific objectives might be:

1. Given a list of words with the prefixes "anti" and "pro," students will be able to explain how the affixed word differs from the root word.

2. Given a paragraph at the student's independent reading level, the student will be able to choose the main idea from a list of four alternatives.

3. Given a set of computations requiring addition without regrouping the student will be able to indicate whether or not the answers are correct.

How Will Students Accomplish the Learning or Develop the Interests That Have Been Identified by the Purpose and Objectives of the Center?

Your next decision concerns what your students should do, i.e., what behaviors they should use, in order to accomplish the learning or develop the interests that have been identified by the objectives and/or purpose.

Learning behaviors which students can use in working with center activities might be placed into two basic categories, or into a combination of these categories. One type of learning behavior deals with receiving information, while a second type of learning behavior relates to expressing or demonstrating information. Many center activities require students to use both types of learning behaviors. Some of the learning behaviors from which you might choose are listed below:

Examples of Learning Behaviors

Those which primarily involve **Receiving Information**	Those which primarily involve **Expressing Information**
Reading	Writing
Listening	Discussing
Observing	Constructing
Examining	Explaining
Viewing	Illustrating
Collecting Data	Reading (orally to convey information)

Those which combine
Receiving and Expressing Information

Experimenting
Interviewing
Critiquing
Contrasting
Estimating
Describing
Comparing
Measuring

Among the factors which you will want to consider in selecting a learning behavior for students to use in working with center activities are these:

- the level of your students' reading achievement,
- their ability to express themselves in writing, and
- the extent to which they are able to perform the specific processes independently.

Oftentimes, new content is introduced best through selecting a learning behavior familiar to students. For example, new content concerning the concept of erosion might be presented through viewing a filmstrip. By introducing new content through a familiar learning behavior, the center builds on students' strengths even though the content included may be unfamiliar.

Teachers often combine two or more learning behaviors, such as listening and discussing, in a center. Many teachers plan centers which enable students to choose from among several behaviors one which they prefer. For example, a student might choose between tape-recording and illustrating his response to a question.

Some examples of learning behaviors include the following:

1. Students listen to the story on the tape and then dramatize their reaction to the story.
2. Students read the paragraphs and then write the main idea of each.
3. Students examine capital and small letters and match them.
4. Students collect data (read-observe) on the extent of pollution in the area and present a "TV newscast" on their findings.

What Materials Will I Use in the Center?

After basic decisions about purpose, objectives, and learning behaviors have been made, it is necessary to select materials to use in the center. In order to make the most efficient use of time and materials, you should determine first if there are commercial (published) materials available for inclusion in the center. Some publishers have produced complete learning centers for students while others have developed materials which are easily adaptable for use in centers. Examine the materials to determine if they will help you accomplish the objectives you have identified for the center through the process/es which you have selected. If the materials appear to be appropriate with regard to objectives and process, study the materials carefully to determine the following information:

1. Do the commercial materials include directions appropriate for independent use by students? If not, can appropriate directions be prepared? (Refer to page 23 for ideas concerning how to make center directions appropriate for independent student use.)

2. Are the materials multi-level in nature? If not, can they be made multi-level? (Refer to page 14 for ideas suggesting ways center activities can be made multi-level.) If the materials are not multi-level, could different commercial materials or teacher-made materials related to the same topic be used to provide variety in levels of difficulty?

3. Are the materials self-correcting? If not, can they be made to be self-correcting? (Refer to page 18 for ideas concerning how to make center activities self-correcting.)

4. Are the commercial materials manipulative? If not, can they be made manipulative? (Refer to page 11 for ideas concerning how to make center activities manipulative.) Commercial materials which teachers frequently have used in centers include:

Commercial Materials		
learning games	workbooks	flannel board and/or magnetic board manipulative materials
kits	pocket charts	
tradebooks	flannel or magnetic boards	
tape recorders		
transparencies	game kits	toys
tapes	filmstrips	puzzles
records	flash cards	picture cards

If appropriate commercial materials are not available, or if the materials cannot be modified for center use, you will need to select other materials for center construction. Among the many types of materials available are these:

Content Materials		
catalogs	application forms	tv guides
food boxes	magazines	posters
newspapers	old workbooks	maps
photos	brochures	pictures
ads	labels	game parts
sports photos		

Construction Materials		
cardboard boxes	heavy cardboard	wallpaper
plastic containers	milk cartons	paint
construction paper	contact paper	cans
popsicle sticks	index cards	glue
glossy-surfaced paper	envelopes	scissors
	tag board	pens
stapler	tape	

How Can I Make the Center Manipulative?

Although center activities which involve writing often are very worthwhile tasks for students, they may react negatively to those centers which require too much writing. Students also may react negatively if all centers that they use require writing. Teachers who have used centers extensively report that students prefer center activities which are manipulative. If you decide to make your center activities manipulative, here are some tips which may help you.

1. Use puzzles for activities such as: matching questions with answers, matching words with their definitions, matching pictures with beginning consonants, or matching words with syllabication patterns.

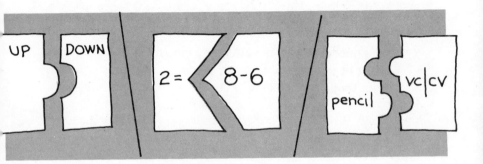

2. Use yarn for activities such as: matching letters, matching related pictures, matching words with pictures, or matching questions with answers.

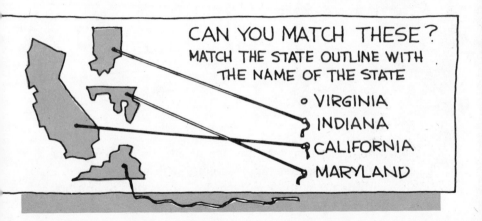

3. Use paper plates and clothespins for activities such as: matching word opposites, matching states and capitals, matching problems with answers.

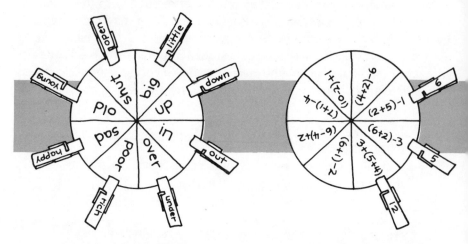

4. Use pocket charts for activities such as: matching pictures with beginning consonants, placing pictures or events in sequence, and placing pictures or words in categories.

5. Mount pictures, captions, words, etc. on cards for activities such as: matching headlines with articles, captions with pictures, titles with stories, words with definitions, and main ideas with paragraphs.

6. Prepare sets of pictures, paragraphs, letters, etc. for activities involving: sequencing, alphabetizing, or categorizing.

7. Use boxes, cans, or banks for activities involving: sorting, classifying, and categorizing.

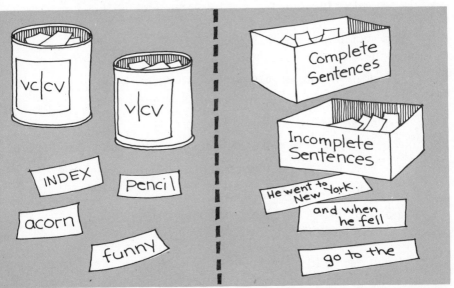

Should I Include More Than One Activity within the Center?
If So, Should I Make the Activities Multi-Level in Difficulty
or Should I Make All Activities at the Same Level of Difficulty?
How Can I Make the Activities Multi-Level?

One of the major decisions you must make in developing a center concerns the number of activities to be included in the center. You may decide that you will need only one activity to accomplish the objectives or fulfill the purpose you have established for the center. If so, it is important to match the difficulty level and interest appeal of that activity with the students who will be using it.

Or, you may decide that you will need more than one activity in your center in order to accomplish the objectives or fulfill the purpose you have established. If so, still another decision needs to be made: (a) will the activities be quite similar with respect to difficulty and learning behaviors involved or (b) will the activities be multi-level, i.e., different with respect to difficulty or learning behaviors involved?

You may want to make the activities quite similar with respect to the level of difficulty or learning behavior involved if:

1. your objectives involve reinforcement of a single skill;
2. students who will be using the center work well with similar learning behaviors; or
3. students who will be using the center are at approximately the same point in their skill development.

You should develop multi-level activities if students who will use the center:

1. differ with respect to level of achievement;
2. have different strengths, needs, and interests; or
3. prefer different learning processes.

You should develop multi-level activities if the center is to feature:

1. more than one skill or concept;
2. a difficult skill or concept; or
3. the introduction and development of an unfamiliar concept or skill.

If you decide to make your center multi-level, several techniques are available. Some of these techniques are presented below. Specific examples of centers which incorporate these techniques are described in the Idea Bank in Chapter 7.

1. Varying the quantity of materials or tasks in an activity can make the activity easier or more difficult. For example, matching six initial consonants with pictures of objects beginning with those consonants (Activity II) is a more difficult task than matching two initial consonants with corresponding pictured objects (Activity I).

Activity I   Activity II

 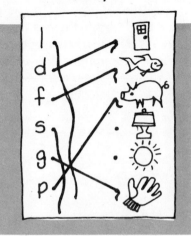

2. Varying the complexity of an activity can make it easier or more difficult. (An activity involving complex tasks is more difficult than an activity involving the same number of simple tasks.) For example, an activity which consists of five subtraction problems which require regrouping is more difficult than an activity which consists of five subtraction problems which do not require regrouping.

Activity I

37	35	68	17	25
-17	-21	-24	-12	-14

Activity II

37	35	68	17	25
-18	-27	-29	- 9	-17

3. Varying the amount of new information included in an activity contributes to its level of difficulty. (An activity which introduces unfamiliar content is more difficult than an activity which reinforces similar familiar content.)

4. Varying the type of learning behaviors involved may make the activity easier or more difficult. (Listening is more simple than reading; reading is less difficult than writing. An activity which requires an oral response is less difficult than the same activity which requires a written response.) In the math example in Number 2 above, both activities could have been made less difficult if students were to match answer cards with the problems rather than writing answers to the problems.

37	35	68	17	25
-17	-21	-24	-12	-14

20   14   44   5   11

An activity in a science center in which a student can use a reference book to locate answers to questions is less difficult than an activity in which the same questions must be answered from memory, or recall.

5. Varying the amount of assistance available to students can make a difference in the difficulty level of an activity. (Activities which must be done independently may be more difficult than activities on which students can work together.) An activity in which two students work together on a data collection project concerning causes of an energy crises may be less difficult than an activity requiring one student to obtain the same data.

6. Varying the extent to which students must consult materials or resources outside the center to complete center activities may contribute to the difficulty of those activities. (Activities which require the student to obtain information from sources not provided in the center may be more difficult than activities requiring students to obtain information from sources provided within the center.) For example, if students are to develop a time line tracing the westward movement of settlers in the United States, it is easier for them to accomplish this task if needed references are available within the center than if students must go to the media center to locate specific information in appropriate sources.

Less Difficult	**More Difficult**
Look in the books below to find the information you need to make the time line.	Go to the media center to find sources containing information you need to make the time line.

7. Varying the number of illustrations can contribute to the difficulty of a center. (Activities which include pictures may be less difficult than those which include only words.) For example, a center activity which involves constructing a relief map from papier mâché would be easier for students to do if directions for constructing the map included illustrations, diagrams, or photographs.

Less Difficult	**More Difficult**

1. Tear paper in small strips.
 	
2. Add: 1 cup flour
 	
   1 T. salt
 	
   ½ cup water
	1. Tear paper in small strips.
	
	2. Add: 1 cup flour
	
	   1 T. salt
	
	   ½ cup water

When they are developing multi-level centers, some teachers prefer to begin with an activity of average difficulty, and then ask; "How can I make it more difficult? How can I make it easier?" Other teachers prefer to plan activities by beginning with the most simple activity and adding more difficult activities in a step-by-step manner. Some teachers plan center activities for a specific group of students, and later include additional activities to make the center appropriate for more students.

Although multi-level centers require more time for planning and development than single activity centers, they may be used by more students for a longer period of time than single activity centers or centers with several activities at the same level.

Should Some Center Activities Be Made Open-Ended?

As you develop centers for your students, include a balance of center activities which are open-ended and center activities which are not open-ended. Open-ended center activities often encourage creativity, stimulate critical thinking, provide opportunities for students to pursue topics or projects of interest to them, and present challenges different from those activities containing tasks with specific correct responses. In addition, open-ended center activities enable students to apply their skills and concepts without the limitations imposed by activities which are not open-ended.

Many center activities can be easily adapted to an open-ended format. For example, a center activity in which students match pictures with appropriate titles and stories could be made open-ended by having students create titles and stories to go with pictures they have collected. This open-ended format provides opportunities for students to select pictures of interest to them, encourages them to draw on their own experiences, and stimulates critical and creative thinking.

Open-ended center activities are appropriate and important for every student — not just the able student and the student who finishes other activities rapidly. Every student should have the opportunity to express his interests and ideas, and demonstrate his skill strengths through open-ended activities. Centers should be planned in a manner which enables all students to become involved with open-ended activities.

How Can Students Evaluate Their Performance with Center Activities?

It is most important for students to receive feedback concerning the center activities. If no feedback is provided, students may reinforce incorrect associations, or they may become discouraged from lack of response to their efforts. In addition, feedback from student work with center activities provides the teacher with diagnostic information useful in adjusting instruction and evaluating student progress. The question is not whether some type of evaluation should be included, but rather, what type of evaluation should be included. Here you have many choices: self-correction, self-evaluation, teacher evaluation, and joint student-teacher evaluation. The nature of the center you are developing may dictate the type of evaluation you decide to use.

1. Self-correction is especially appropriate when activities have one correct answer. Students are able to obtain immediate feedback, correct any errors they have made, and reinforce correct associations. Teachers have used several different techniques to make centers self-correcting. Among these techniques are:

   ● Separate answer keys

   > Answer cards, sheets, or other types of keys might be prepared for each activity, and appropriately coded. These cards might be kept in an answer file box, in separate envelopes, or might be inserted within the center itself.

   ● Color coding

   > Color coding is especially appropriate when the center includes activities which involve matching and categorizing. Small colored circles, dots, or symbols may be used.

   ● Number or Letter coding

   > Number or letter coding is useful when the center includes activities which involve matching, sequencing, or categorizing.

   ● Picture coding

   > Picture coding might be used with young children.

   ● Puzzle format

   > Puzzle formats are appropriate for any type of matching activity and some sequencing activities. Items that are to be matched are placed on puzzle pieces which fit together when matched appropriately.

- Covered answers

  Answers might be included within the activity, but might be covered by flaps or small pictures which conceal them.

- Answers on reverse side of activity

  Answers may be listed on the back of the paper, chart, folder, or other material on which the activity is presented.

- Separate keys

  Some students prefer separate answer keys to answers provided within the center. Conferences with students enable them to express preferences and reasons for their preferences.

2. Self-evaluation is a desirable evaluation strategy in several situations. You may prefer to use self-evaluation when there is more than one correct answer possible for center activities, or when center activities are open-ended. When you want to know how students feel about the tasks they have accomplished, self-evaluation strategies may be used. Self-evaluation is very appropriately applied to centers when there are specific aspects of student efforts on which you want students to focus, e.g., margins, neatness. In addition, you may find self-evaluation particularly relevant when the center is one which developes interests rather than introduces or reinforces concepts and skills. Specific examples of self-evaluation techniques include writing a reaction statement, drawing a smiling or frowning face to indicate a reaction, or discussing a reaction with a teacher in a conference situation.

3. Teacher evaluation may be used for any type of center activity, but it is especially appropriate when activities may have more than one correct answer, when a creative product has been developed, or when students need feedback in addition to self-correction and self-evaluation. Two disadvantages involved with teacher evaluation are (a) increased demand for teacher-time, and (b) greater possibility of delayed feedback.

4. Teacher-student evaluation (conferences) provides an excellent opportunity for teachers to obtain diagnostic information concerning student progress with skills presented in centers, and offers students the opportunity to obtain assistance, ask questions, and make suggestions. Many teachers like to schedule small group conferences with students who have similar strengths and needs. Such conferences often indicate the need for teachers to use flexible grouping strategies for reinforcement of specific content or skills.

Teachers who have used centers most successfully have conference time planned daily. Conferences may vary in length and frequently group conferences can be scheduled. Conferences may be held at the teacher's desk, at students' desks or tables, in areas where small group instruction usually occurs, or at the location of the center itself. Every child does not need a conference every day. The important point is that the teacher should be available for "conferencing" when students need to hold a conference with the teacher. Teacher-student evaluation done through "conferencing" is often used in addition to other types of evaluation.

How Shall I Package or Display the Center?

Several factors must be considered when you select a means of packaging or displaying a center.

- How much space is available for displaying centers and working with center activities?
- What type of activities are students going to be doing?
- Can the centers remain in one area, or must they be moved from room to room?
- How many students will be using the center activities?

Here are some of the techniques for packaging and displaying center activities which have been used successfully by teachers.

Learning Centers : A Guide for Effective Use

If your space is quite limited, or if you must move your centers from one room to another, you might consider packaging the activities in folders, manila envelopes, notebooks, or small boxes, so that students can work at centers at a convenient location.

If several students are to use a center at one time, you might display the activities on a large bulletin board, carton, table, or chart.

Remember that students respond well to variety, so consider using a number of different packaging or display techniques for your centers.

How Do I Prepare Directions for the Center and Then Communicate These Directions to Students?

Clear, thorough, well planned directions assist students to use center activities independently. Some suggestions to help you prepare directions for centers are listed below.

1. Make the directions clear and legible.

   - Write or type directions with care, and use ample margins. If several students will be using the center at one time, be certain that the print is sufficiently large and dark. Space the directions so they can be seen easily.

   - When appropriate, enumerate the directions and underline key words.

2. Use terminology familiar to students.

   - Because students will be using the center activities independently, it is important that students can recognize the words used in the directions, and that they know what these words mean.

3. Use audio-visual aids to help students understand directions.

   - Directions may be placed on tape. If students have difficulty reading printed directions, taped directions may enable them to work independently. Some teachers prefer taping directions so that they can explain concepts or offer examples. Other teachers use the tape recorder to tape center activities as well as the directions. Students with a strong auditory learning modality may respond especially well to taped directions.

- Sketches or photographs may be used to clarify written or taped directions. These visual aids would be useful for very young students, students experiencing reading difficulty, or any students who might need written directions clarified.

- A chart presenting and illustrating key directional terms is a useful reference for many students. For example, the terms such as: "cut," "paste," "circle," or "draw" might be included with appropriate illustrations, on a reference chart for beginning readers.

4. Include examples of tasks to be accomplished, when appropriate. In order to work independently, students may need a few examples which illustrate the type of task to be completed. For instance, if words are to be divided into syllables, examples illustrating how this task should be done may be quite helpful for students.

5. Include enough organizational information in the directions to enable students to work independently. It might be appropriate to include some of the following information:

- the center number or other identifying symbol.
- the number of students who can work with that center at one time.
- where the activities are to be completed, e.g., at a desk, at a table.
- what is to be done with finished products developed in the center.
- what type of record-keeping information is needed.
- what type of evaluation will be done.
- where reference materials can be obtained, if needed.
- where to obtain assistance.

It is important that students clearly understand this organizational information before they begin to use the center. A "dry run" is necessary in assuring that this type of information is clear to students.

6. Include the objective and/or purpose for the center. It is important for students to know why they are doing a given center activity. If objectives are included, the student, as part of his self-evaluation, can determine if he has met the objectives for the center. Objectives may be included in the written directions, or may be explained to students.

7. Include information about evaluation. Directions should state what type of evaluation is to be used for the center activities. If the activities are not self-correcting, the directions should indicate what students should do when they have completed the activities. It may be helpful to include what students are to do if they have difficulty with the activities.

8. Evaluate your directions. Carefully review the directions you have prepared for the center. Will students be able to read the directions without difficulty? After they read the directions, will they know:

- What they are to do?

- Why they are to do it?

- How they are to accomplish the tasks involved?

- How their work will be evaluated?

If your answers to all of these questions are "yes," the students for whom the center is designed should be able to use it independently.

9. "Dry run" center activities with a small group of students to pinpoint potential problems with the activities.

10. Explain or "dry run" center directions with all students who will be using the center.

11. Assign a "center buddy" to the center in order to help other students to read and interpret directions.

How Can I Save Time in Developing Centers?

Although center development is a very challenging project, it also can be a very time-consuming project. Here are some tips to save time for you when you are developing centers:

1. Make centers durable for reuse.

   - Use clear contact paper to cover parts of center materials. The contact paper makes the materials durable, easy to clean, and attractive.

   - Laminate center materials to make them sturdy, and easy to clean.

   - Mount papers or pictures to add strength and durability to these easily torn materials.

   - Use acetate covers to protect papers, pictures, workbook pages or other easily torn materials used in centers. Students can write on the acetate since it may be cleaned easily with a cloth or tissue.

   - Use small boxes and plastic bags to keep small parts and pieces from getting lost.

2. Construct centers with activities which may be modified to keep them current and relevant.

   - Retain the basic center format, but change specific materials such as: pictures, books, or worksheets used within it.

   - Retain the basic center format, but add appropriate activities.

   - Retain the basic center format and materials, but change the directions.

   - Construct center backgrounds or formats which can be used appropriately for several different skill activities within a grade or teaching team or across grades or teams. For example, a general center background featuring horses (Galloping Along With . . .) might be used to reinforce third grade spelling skills as well as third grade math skills.

A "Sherlock Holmes" background (Find the Answer) may be used in a third grade math center on fractions as well as a fifth grade math center on decimals.

BASIC BACKGROUND

Many different topics could be used.

Many different levels of math activities could be used.

3. Work with a friend or teammate.

- Trade centers with another teacher if the centers are appropriate for both groups of students.

- Make two centers with identical activities . . . one for you and one for a colleague whose students have needs similar to those of your students. Your colleague does the same for you.

- Work with colleagues while you are constructing centers. Colleagues can offer assistance with ideas, assembling materials, etc.

4. Plan for proper storage so centers can be reused.

- Store large center activities in portfolios of appropriate size.

- Use large cartons to store centers containing many types of materials.

- Use files for folder-type centers or small center activities.

- Label storage files, boxes, and portfolios for rapid location of center activities.

5. Set aside an area for construction or equip a large box with all needed construction tools. If supplies such as: tape, scissors, stapler, contact paper, and pens are housed in a convenient location, time which may have been spent collecting materials can be used for constructing centers.

6. Have the basic center "blueprint" clearly in mind before construction begins. If purpose and objectives have been established, and decisions concerning levels, directions, and type of correction have been made, center construction can proceed much more rapidly. Time spent in careful planning means less time spent in construction.

7. Get parents to help. Volunteer parents can construct centers which you have planned and sketched. For most satisfactory results, carefully plan and outline the center before having parents construct it. Be certain to discuss considerations such as legibility of print, margins, durability, and clarity with parents who are constructing materials for you.

8. Get students to help with center planning and construction. Students will enjoy having the opportunity to assist you, and they will feel more personally involved with the completed center activities. Students might help with activities such as:

- locating pictures
- assembling
- cutting

- printing
- pasting
- painting.

Students also may be involved with modifying existing centers and planning new ones in cooperation with the teacher. Students might identify high interest topics or appealing activities which could become part of centers used in instruction. You may wish to set aside a specific time each week in which students may work on planning or constructing centers.

9. Locate consumable workbooks, dittos, old texts, pictures, magazine articles, and other materials that relate to topics to be featured in centers. These materials can be placed in a convenient location for use when needed.

10. Use commercially prepared materials whenever appropriate. (See page 8 for a discussion of using commercial materials in centers.)

11. When you do not have time to construct a center but you do have a good idea and some "parts and pieces," prepare an envelope for each center idea. On the front of each envelope, jot down the center purpose, sample directions, construction ideas, and any other related information. Within the envelope, place parts and pieces which you collect for constructing the center. If you have a snapshot of a similar center you have seen at a workshop or in a classroom, include it in the envelope for future reference.

Organization and Management

When should I use centers in my classroom?
How do I organize my classroom and my curriculum when I am using centers?
How can I help students to work independently?
How do I keep records when I am using centers?

One of the keys to successful use of learning centers is developing strategies for efficient center organization and management that work for you.

How will you use the centers? When will they be used? How will you organize your centers? Will you assign students to centers, or will centers be selected by students? These are some of the decisions you will need to make when you use centers.

When Should I Use Centers in My Classroom?

One of the major advantages learning centers offer is the flexibility with which they can be used. Centers may be used to supplement the curriculum, they may be used as an integral part of the curriculum, or they may be used as the basis for organizing the curriculum.

- Centers as a supplement to the curriculum

  Teachers often begin using centers by including them as a supplement to the curriculum. When used in this way, it is essential that care be taken to see that centers are not viewed as "frills," as "punitive requirements," or as additional work. If centers are introduced as a supplement to the curriculum, they should be used in a positive, relevant manner. The following are two examples illustrating the use of centers.

Example I
Teacher Directed Activity --- Non-Center Activities

Group	Time			
	9:30-10:00	10:00-10:30	10:30-11:00	11:00-11:30
A	Teacher Directed Activity	Non-Center Activities* / Learning Centers when finished	Non-Center Activities / Learning Centers when finished	Teacher Directed Activity
B	Non-Center Activities / Learning Centers when finished	Teacher Directed Activity	Non-Center Activities / Learning Centers when finished	Teacher Directed Activity
C	Non-Center Activities / Learning Centers when finished	Non-Center Activities / Learning Centers when finished	Teacher Directed Activity	Teacher Directed Activity

* Non-center activities refer to activities such as workbook
assignments, dittoed pages or chalkboard projects.

In Example I, the teacher works with small or large groups while
other students use non-center activities. After students have finished
assigned non-center activities, they may select a learning center.

One of the problems encountered by teachers who have used
Example I as an organizational strategy involves the slower paced student who is unable to complete his non-center activities in time to
work with learning centers. In assisting the slower paced student, you
should be certain that his non-center activities are appropriate for
him. Have conferences with him to help him plan his time wisely, and
consider assigning centers in place of some of his other activities.

Example II
Teacher Directed Activity --- Non-Center Activities --- Scheduled Center Tir

Group	Time				
	9:30-10:00	10:00-10:30	10:30-11:00	11:00-11:30	11:3(12:0(
A	Teacher Directed Activity	Non-Center Activities*	Non-Center Activities	Teacher Directed Activity	C E
B	Non-Center Activities	Teacher Directed Activity	Non-Center Activities	Teacher Directed Activity	N T E
C	Non-Center Activities	Non-Center Activities	Teacher Directed Activity	Teacher Directed Activity	R S

* Non-center activities refer to activities such as workbook assignments, dittoed pages or chalkboard projects.

In Example II, a special, separate "center time" is set aside on specific days. During the center time, all students work with centers while the teacher is available to offer assistance when needed. The period set aside for center time might be brief or extensive, depending on the number of centers available, the experience of the students in working independently, and the purpose for which the centers are being used.

The center time might be scheduled daily, weekly, or at whatever interval appears to be most convenient.

Example II is also applicable to situations in which centers are used as an integral part of the curriculum.

- Centers as an integral part of the curricular program

    Centers are frequently used as an integral part of the curriculum along with teacher directed activities and traditional seatwork or workbook activities. The following are some examples of this type of organization.

Example III
Teacher Directed Activity --- Center Activity --- Seatwork/Workbook

Group	Time					
	9:30-10:00	10:00-10:30	10:30-11:00	11:00-11:30	11:30-12:00	
A	Teacher Directed Activity	Non-Center Activities*	Centers	Teacher Directed Activity	Non-Center Activities	C O N F E R E N C E S
B	Centers	Teacher Directed Activity	Non-Center Activities	Teacher Directed Activity	Centers	
C	Non-Center Activities	Centers	Teacher Directed Activity	Teacher Directed Activity	Centers	

* Non-center activities refer to activities such as workbook
assignments, dittoed pages or chalkboard projects.

In Example III, students might be involved in teacher directed activities, in workbook/seatwork activities, or in center activities. Variations of this model could be used for one area of the curriculum, or for several curriculum areas. This example illustrates the type of flexible grouping which is possible when centers are used in the classroom.

In one time period, the teacher is working with the entire group in a teacher directed activity. During another period, the teacher is holding conferences with some students while others work with centers or non-center activities. During other periods, the teacher is working with one group while other groups work in centers or with workbook activities.

Example IV
Teacher Directed Activity --- Center Activity

Group	Time					
	9:30-10:00	10:00-10:30	10:30-11:00	11:00-11:30		
A	Teacher Directed Activity	Centers	Centers	Centers	T E A C H E R	C O N F E R E N C E S
B	Centers	Teacher Directed Activity	Centers	Centers		
C	Centers	Centers	Teacher Directed Activity	Centers		

In Example IV, students are involved either with teacher directed activities or with center activities. The students use centers in place of assigned seatwork activities. Variations of this model could be used for one area of the curriculum, such as language arts, or for several areas of the curriculum. It might be applied to team teaching situations as well as non-teamed situations.

- Centers as a basis for organizing the curriculum

    When centers are used as the basis for organizing the curriculum, most instruction is introduced and reinforced through centers. Teachers plan and develop centers, assist students with center activities, hold conferences with individual students and small groups of students and do some large and small group instruction. If centers are used as the basis for organizing the curriculum, a daily schedule may look like this:

Example V
Center Activity --- Teacher Conference

9:30-11:00	11:00-12:30	1:30-3:00
Language Arts Centers	Math Centers	Science and Social Studies Centers
Conferences, large group and small group teacher directed activities scheduled as needed.		

(Classes such as art, music, and physical education would be scheduled within this organizational framework.)

Centers might be used as the basis for organizing specific aspects of the curriculum such as language arts, or mathematics, while teacher directed activities would be used as the basis for organizing other aspects of the curriculum.

Any combination of these organizational examples might be used successfully. For example, some teachers have used Example II three days a week, and Example IV two days a week.

After you have determined how centers fit into your curriculum, it is helpful to establish a system to inform students when they may use centers. The procedure you select will depend to some extent upon your overall strategy for using centers. If you are combining use of centers with both teacher directed activities and non-center activities, it will help to have a time schedule for students to follow. Here are some suggestions:

1. Use a Time Schedule.

   Establish daily plans with students such as those below:

       9:00 - 9:15 -- Opening
       9:15 - 10:45 -- Reading and Center Work

Group	Mrs. Smith	Centers
Tom's Group	9:15 - 9:45	9:45 - 10:45
Mary's Group	9:45 - 10:15	9:15 - 9:45 10:15 - 10:45
Ted's Group	10:15 - 10:45	9:15 - 10:15

       10:45 - 11:00 -- Conferences   11:45 -------------- Lunch
       11:00 - 11:45 -- Math   etc.

2. Use a Topic Schedule.

   Students consult the chart to determine where they should be working. The teacher changes the chart as classroom activities change.

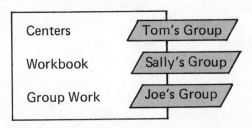

   Centers   Tom's Group
   Workbook   Sally's Group
   Group Work   Joe's Group

If your curriculum is organized around centers with teacher conferences, it is important to develop a conference schedule. Some teachers prepare a list of conference times, and indicate which students are to meet for conferences during these times. Other teachers prepare a time schedule, but have students sign up for conferences when they feel they are ready. You may prefer to combine the techniques described above by scheduling some conference times but having students sign up for others. When students are not involved in a conference or scheduled group activity, they are involved with center activities. For information concerning times during which students may obtain assistance with center activities, see page 47.

How Shall I Organize the Centers I Develop?

Choosing a procedure for organizing your centers helps to make the use of centers more successful and efficient.

Teachers are using several types of organizational strategies for their centers.

1. Coding Centers with Numbers or Letters

   Each center is assigned a number or letter. Assignment of centers can be done through reference to the center letter or number. Within the center, activities might be numbered or lettered. Using a coding system such as this enables students and teacher to refer to specific centers and center activities with relative ease. "Activity C in Center number 7" can be identified clearly by everyone.

2. Color Coding Centers

   Many teachers color code their centers and some use color coding in conjunction with a numbering or lettering system. Color coding is done in several ways:

   - All centers dealing with a specific area of the curriculum to which it related might be assigned the same color. For example, math centers might be coded green; language arts centers, red; social studies centers, blue; etc.

   - All centers dealing with a specific topic or skill might be assigned the same color. For example, all centers dealing with identifying main idea might be coded with a specific color.

   - Color coding might indicate the complexity of activities within a center when centers include more than one activity. For example, those activities coded blue might be beginning level activities, those activities coded red might be somewhat more complex, and those activities coded brown might be the most complex of all. This information would be useful to students when they are selecting center activities.

Not all children would need to begin with the least complex activities, and no child would stay at a specific color level. Rather, children would select an initial activity at their level of competency, and move through the activities at their own pace.

It is important to note that the color coding refers to the complexity of the activity, not to the ability level of the child.

3. Skill/Objective Coding of Centers

Many teachers who stress diagnostic-prescriptive teaching prefer to organize their centers on the basis of the skills or objectives upon which instruction within the classroom, team area, or school is based. Skill/objective coding is also a desirable organizational alternative when a school as a whole develops a large number of centers for use throughout the school.

To organize centers by skills or objectives, the teacher or staff first would identify and list those specific skills and objectives around which instruction is based. As centers are developed, each center is assigned a number. A master chart or set of file cards is prepared upon which each skill or objective is listed, along with the numbers of those centers which introduce or reinforce that skill. Many centers would be appropriate for more than one objective or skill. This master chart or file system can be made available to all teachers and updated as new centers are developed.

Example of Card from Diagnostic-Prescriptive Center File

Objective: Students can identify words which rhyme and state additional rhyming words.

Centers: 6, 10, 20, 43, 71, 72, 80.

Many teachers like to keep a center notebook in which each center they develop is described and coded. If the actual center is consumed, the coded idea remains available in the notebook for future reference.

Should Students Select Centers or Should Center Activities be Assigned?

Most teachers decide to combine student self-selection of centers with teacher assignment of centers.

Here are some of the factors you will want to consider in reaching a decision concerning self-selection of centers:

- the number of centers available,
- the number of multi-level centers available,
- the instructional objectives of the centers,
- the purpose for which the centers were developed,
- the amount of experience students have had with self-selection,
- the manner in which students handle self-direction,
- the strengths, needs, and interests of your students.

Total free choice, or total self-selection of centers is recommended when students have learned the skills of self-selection and self-direction, and can assess independently whether or not a center is appropriate for their purposes. Total self-selection also may be used when any center would be appropriate for students.

Guided self-selection is recommended when teachers have developed centers to meet the needs of specific students, when some centers are appropriate for some students but not for all students, when students have little experience with self-selection and self-direction, when diagnostic information indicates that students would profit from working with specific center activities, or when the sequence of center activities is an important consideration.

Guided self-selection does not imply that teachers must tell students which centers to use and when to use them. Instead, teachers give just enough assistance to help students make appropriate decisions. Guidance should encourage and assist students with independent decision making.

Here are some examples of how guided self-selection might work:

- Students might select one or more centers from a group of centers recommended by the teacher. For example, the teacher might say, "Centers number 6, number 8, and number 10 could help you practice using an index. Choose one of the three to do today."

- Students might select one or more activities within an assigned center. For example, the teacher might say, "Any of the activities in Center number 7 could help you with locating root words. Choose one or more of the activities to do today."

- Students might decide in which order or at what time to complete assigned centers. For example, the teacher might say, "Sometime this week, work with the activities in Center number 6 and Center number 2. These activities will help you identify main idea." Or, "Today, I'd like you to go to the centers listed on the chart beside your name. You can do the centers in any order you prefer." Additional information concerning guided self-selection is discussed in Chapter 6.

You may decide that students should have total free choice in selecting some centers but should be given guidance in selecting others. You may also decide that some students need more guidance with self-selection than others. If some students experience great difficulty with self-selection, you may wish to guide their selection carefully or assign a buddy to work with that student to help him select an appropriate center.

Help students with self-selection. To help students select appropriate centers, you may wish to plan some teacher directed lessons dealing with the process of selecting centers. You might "role play" with students a situation in which they are to choose a center to help them with word attack skills. Discuss each center with the group, encouraging them to identify why the center would be a good choice or why it would be an inappropriate choice. Students might develop a set of questions to ask themselves when they select a center. For example, they might ask,

1. "Is this center about something I am studying?"
2. "Will this center help me with something I am learning?"
3. "Can I do the activities in this center?"

It is also important to help students to evaluate how effective their selection of centers has been, and to help them to assess how well they planned their center activities. You might guide them to ask questions such as these:

1. "Was I able to do the center activities I selected?"
2. "Did I choose too many center activities?"
3. "Could I have done more center activities?"
4. "Did I check my work?"
5. "Do I need a conference with the teacher?"

These suggestions can help you move gradually from total teacher guidance to a great deal of total self-selection. Through guiding student self-selection, you give students appropriate alternatives from which to select activities which meet their interests and needs. As students demonstrate ability to select centers within the guidelines you establish, you can increase opportunities for them to select centers independently.

Remember, too, that self-selection is made possible when you provide alternatives for students which are based on instructional objectives developed from diagnostic information. When these types of activities are made available, students have an opportunity for decision making in a situation in which teachers can be accountable for instruction.

Several alternatives for organizing teacher guided self-selection are presented below:

1. A master chart might be devised which lists each student's name. Beside the name of the student, the teacher would indicate which centers that student should use.

Chart I

Name	Day				
	Monday	Tuesday	Wednesday	Thursday	Friday
Bill	1, 2, 4-A	4-B, 10	5, 7-A, B		
Joe	3, 6-C	6-D	4-B, 10		
Ted	4-B, 5-A	3, 7-B	7-C		
Jane	4-C, 3	7-B	7-C		

According to Chart I, on Monday, Bill is to do Center number 1, Center number 2, and activity A in Center number 4. Joe is to do Center number 3 and C in Center number 6, and so on. Assignments for the remainder of the week have not been made. The teacher might assign additional centers later in the week based upon student performance on Monday, Tuesday, and Wednesday, or students might self-select centers for Thursday and Friday.

2. A master chart might be devised which lists each center by name or number. Student name cards can be inserted beside the appropriate center number. It is important for the teacher to indicate the maximum number of students who can work at a center at any given time.

Center Title or Number	Student's Name	Number of Students Who Can Work at Center
Place Value (5)	Ted Jane Ann	3
Homonyms (23)	Bill Sam Joe Bob	4
Measurement (15)	Ron Lea	2

3. Name cards of students who are to use a center might be placed near that center. (Commercially produced assignment boards may be adapted for this purpose.)

4. Individual "mail boxes" might be used for center assignment. The student would pick up his assignment from his mailbox at times designated by the teacher.

Joe, do center 7 and 6-B today. Mrs. Smith	Ann, you may do any of the "red" activities in Centers 4, 10 and 6 today.

5. Assignment might be made through conferences with the teacher. Teachers could indicate during the conference which centers students should use. Directions could be presented orally or in writing.

6. Contracting is a technique used by many teachers to assist the student in decision-making concerning the centers he is to use. The teacher and the student negotiate which centers will be done, how much time is to be used, how progress will be demonstrated, and how the student's work will be evaluated. The student might come to the contracting conference with a form filled out in this manner.

I will complete the following centers by ___*January 15*___

Signed ___*Rodney*___

Approved ___(teacher signs here)___

Check here if you plan to complete a given center	Center Number	Center Name	Comment
_____	4	Fractions	_____
____✓____	2	Syllabication	_____
_____	3	Creative Writing	_____
____✓____	10	Map Making	_____
____✓____	21	Reading Labels	_____
_____	_____	(Student might add a center not on the list.)	_____

During the conference the teacher and the student discuss the appropriateness of his choices, whether or not he is pacing himself wisely, and how he plans to comment on his work. This form then becomes the record of the agreement, of the work completed, and the evaluation.

Usually, when a student contracts for activities and is successful in his efforts, some acknowledgement of this success is forthcoming. New contracts are negotiated based on performance with previous ones.*

7. Assignment of students to centers when centers are organized by skill/objective might be done through following a procedure such as the one below:

a. Determine what skills students need to develop through conferences, informal assessment, or other diagnostic teaching strategies.

b. List this skill, along with the code number of appropriate centers, on a prescription card, contract, or planning sheet for the student.

c. Assess whether the student has mastered the skill through appropriate diagnostic strategies.

Name: Johnny

Date: April 3

Practice rhyming words at Centers 6, 10, or 20.

---

8. Many teachers find it helpful to use a pretest-post test system to assist with guided self-selection. A pretest-post test system can be used to determine:

a. if a specific center is appropriate for a student.

b. which activities within a center are most appropriate for a student.

c. with which center activity a student should begin working.

d. if students have developed the skills or mastered the concepts presented in the center.

Pretests and post tests can be designed for each center and filed for future use. Frequently, pretests can serve as post tests. Both pretests and post tests should reflect the specific nature of the center objectives.

---

* Linda B. Gambrell and Robert M. Wilson, "Contracting - One Way to Individualize," Elementary English, March, 1973, pp. 427-444.

How Can I Keep Records When I Am Using Centers?

An essential aspect of organizing the curriculum for use of centers is provision for student and teacher record-keeping. Students can keep records which include:

- which centers they have used,
- when they have used the centers,
- which activities within the center they have used.

Consideration of the age and ability of your students will help you select an appropriate device for record-keeping.

Examples of several record-keeping devices are described below. Teachers should select the device or combination of devices best suited for their needs.

1. Make multiple copies of a sheet containing a list of students' names. A sheet can be attached to each center in the classroom.

Sample Student Record Sheet

Name	Center _____
Joe	
Mary	
Jim	
George	
Betty	

After students use the center, they might record the following types of information:

Example A

Name	Center _7_
Joe	A--3/7, B--3/9
Mary	A--3/8, B--3/10

Example B

Name	Center _7_
Joe	✓✓
Mary	✓

The information in Example A indicates that Joe did activity A on March 7, and activity B on March 9. Mary did activity A on March 8, and activity B on March 10.

The information in Example B indicates that Joe worked at the center twice, and Mary worked at the center one time.

2. If most of your centers contain more than one activity, you might design a record-keeping sheet such as the one below. Make several copies of the sheet so you can attach one to each center. Students who use this sheet record their name, and list the day in which each activity was completed.

Sample Student Record Sheet

Name	Center _____			
	Activity			
	A	B	C	D

Example C

Name	Center 10			
	Activity			
	A	B	C	D
John	3/7	3/8		
Grace	3/10			
Sue	3/7	3/7	3/7	3/7
Larry			3/8	

The information in Example C indicates that Center number 10 has 4 activities, A, B, C, and D. John completed activity A on March 7 and activity B on March 8. Grace completed activity A on March 10. Sue completed all the activities on the same day, and Larry began with activity C on March 8.

Because the record-keeping devices shown in the examples above are somewhat "public" in nature, the information which students record on them should not be private or personal. Appropriate information for group record-keeping charts might include indications of which centers or center activities are to be used, or have been used and when the activities have been completed.

Grades or student feelings about their efforts should be placed on private records only.

Care should be taken not to use these devices as competitive charts, nor to compare student performance on the basis of the information recorded on them.

3. Individual records can be kept by students. Here is a sample sheet on which a student could list each center completed, when it was completed, and his comments about the center. The sheet might form a daily or weekly record, depending upon the extent of center use. These records are shared only with the teacher.

Sample Student Record Sheet

		Name _____
		Date _____
Center	Date Completed	Comments

Example D

		Name Joe Smith
		Date January 24-27
Center	Date Completed	Comments
1	Jan. 25	I wrote two stories and had Billy read them. The topics were fun.
2	Jan. 25	I had trouble with activity B and I need help. I got three wrong.
3	Jan. 27	I didn't finish activity D. I could do it all O.K.

Example E

Center	Comments
Name	Jane Doe
Date	January 20-24
A	☹
B	☺
C	☺

In Example D, Joe has written comments about his performance with center activities. In Example E, Jane, a first grader, has used smiling and frowning faces to evaluate her work with the centers.

If students have difficulty with a center activity, they may indicate their desire for assistance on their record-keeping sheet. However, since more immediate assistance is oftentimes needed and desirable, teachers have found these suggestions helpful:

a. Schedule a session after each period of time in which centers are used for students to obtain help if needed. This help may be given to individuals or small groups.

b. Schedule a session at the end of each day in which students may obtain help individually or in small group situations.

c. Plan for students to obtain assistance "on the spot" from a previously identified center helper or buddy, see page 51.

d. Devise a system (or procedure) whereby students can get immediate teacher assistance through raising their hands, or by going to a specific location within the instructional area. Some teachers set aside specific times when students may request help in this manner. The important factor is to discuss these procedures with the students beforehand.

e. Schedule periodic sessions in which students have the opportunity to discuss -- as a group -- their reactions to, suggestions for, and thoughts about using learning centers.

Sample Student Record Sheet

Planning Sheet					
Area: Language Arts		Name: _____			
		Date: _____			
Center	Center Objective	Centers Planned	Date Completed	Students' Comments	Teachers' Comments
1	Match Words and Definitions				
12	Locate Information in Index				
14	Locate Information in Telephone Book				
17	Alphabetize Words Using Second Letter				
21	Use Guide Words to Locate Words				
22	Identify Descriptive Words				
25	Divide Words into Syllables				
40	Write a Story				

Prepared in advance by teacher	Teacher and/or student decision	Student	Teacher

When preparing planning sheets such as the one illustrated above, the teacher would:

a. List all centers available for student use. This listing might be done by center number or center name. Only one list needs to be compiled since all available centers are included. Prepare one copy for each student who will be using the learning centers.

b. Beside each center name or number, list the objective(s) for that center. (Use language students can understand!)

c. Include a column for teachers and/or students to check which centers are planned.

d. Include columns for students to record date of center completion and comments.

e. Include a column for teacher comments.

Planning sheets might be organized on the basis of a curriculum area, e.g., language arts; a specific unit, e.g., the Westward Movement; or might include all centers available at a given time.

4. Teacher record-keeping is essential. Examples of records which teachers might keep include:

a. conference notes.

b. skills checklist based on student responses to center activity.

c. copies of record sheets which indicate these data:

- names of students who used a center,
- dates when students used a center,
- response of students to center.

The data which teachers obtain from conferences and records can be used diagnostically to plan future centers and teacher directed activities. The information students receive from conferences and record-keeping can help them grow in self-direction and self-evaluation.

It is most crucial not to confuse record-keeping with grading. Record-keeping should result in more effective teacher planning and more purposeful self-direction on the part of students.

What General Tips for Organization and Management Have Teachers Found Helpful?

Here are some general suggestions for helping you organize center use effectively.

1. Consider the effect placement of centers in the classroom has on student use of centers. If all centers are placed in the same area of the classroom, a student may have difficulty selecting and using centers due to "traffic jams" which result from many students trying to work or move in one small area. If centers are placed throughout the classroom, it may be easier for students to select and work with them.

2. Consider the traffic patterns in your classroom. Location of doors, cabinets, areas for teacher directed activities, and chalkboards may indicate places to avoid in locating centers. Try to keep active areas and quiet study areas as far apart as possible.

3. If your classroom is small, consider packaging many of your center activities compactly, e.g., in folders, envelopes, or small boxes. You may wish to make the centers portable so students can use them at their desks rather than in a central location. Use bulletin boards, sides of cabinets, and book shelves for efficient use of limited space.

4. Limit the number of students who work with centers at any one time if it is difficult for you to have many students involved with center activities at the same time.

5. Enlist the assistance of parent volunteers and older "student aides" to assist students with center activities. Aides and volunteers can assist students with center activities while you conduct teacher directed activities or conferences.

   Before parents or older student aides begin to assist students with center activities, you may wish to schedule an orientation session for them in which you explain your philosophy about centers along with your organization and management techniques. It would be helpful for these aides to observe students working with centers in the classroom before they actually become involved in offering assistance. In addition, it is recommended that you schedule periodic planning sessions in which you and your parent or student aides discuss the progress students are making with center activities, and problems they are encountering with them.

6. Assign center helpers to each center, or to a specific number of centers which you have identified as more difficult than others. Assigning student center helpers to each center in your classroom can help with efficient management of center use. The student center helpers would have these responsibilities:

   a. They study center directions and activities so that they become "experts" in the use of that center. The teacher might work closely with them to assist them to gain this "expertise." And the teacher would take care to assign helpers to centers that would be appropriate for them.

   b. They assist peers with the center when their peers encounter difficulty with directions or specific tasks.

   c. They check to be certain that the center is intact and neatly put away at the end of the center activity period or at the end of the day.

   d. They notify the teacher of any lost, or damaged parts and pieces, and assist in repairing damaged centers.

   The center helpers assist their peers and their teacher while at the same time, assume and develop responsibility.

7. Use student questions about work in centers diagnostically to determine if more assistance is needed with orga-

nizational and procedural matters. For example, if students are asking questions such as the ones below, they may need general teacher assistance in using centers before they can work independently.

"Where do I work?"

"Where do I put my paper?"

"Am I finished?"

"Can Billy help me?"

"What should I do next?"

Many alternatives and options are available to teachers in planning efficient center organization and management. You have an extremely important decision-making role in determining how you will use centers, when they will be used, how your centers will be organized, how students will select centers, and how records will be kept. It is necessary that you choose those options that work best for you in your situation. Do not hesitate to combine, modify, or depart from suggestions offered here and, perhaps most important, seek reactions and suggestions from your students.

Chapter 4

Getting Started

How do I get started with centers?

If you are interested in getting started with centers, here are some suggestions which may assist you. The most important thing to remember is that you are going to be trying learning centers, so take care not to over-commit yourself. Let students and parents know that you think centers may be an effective way to increase student interest and involvement in learning, and that you will be asking for feedback and evaluating your procedures as you go along.

Guidelines for Getting Started

- Begin with reinforcement activities. Many students finish assigned work ahead of others, and teachers frequently are concerned with what to have them do. Learning centers are one answer. Develop centers which have high interest appeal and use them as reinforcement activities for the work which has gone before. You might start with four or five centers which reinforce an area in which you have just completed instruction.

- Set the time or conditions when centers can be used. For example, centers might be used in the morning between 10 and noon, or after assigned activities are completed. When they begin to use centers, some teachers find it useful to schedule several small units of time for center work in order to assist students to become self-directed learners.

- Go over rules with students. Since centers are self-directing activities and since self-direction is learned, the use of centers must be taught. Rules help, especially if there are not too many of them. Let students help set the rules concerning the time when centers are to be used; how many students can work on one center at a time, and where centers are to be used. Some teachers have found it valuable to "dry-run" centers which are new to students so that the students might know what to expect. For example, if a student were to use center A, what steps would he follow? If he ran into trouble, where could he go for help? How does he know if he has finished the activity? What should he do when he completes the activity?

- Help students budget time wisely. Students might be presented with decisions such as this: If you choose to work on center A, what consequences might occur? Will you develop more skill with center A activities? Will you have less time for free reading?

- Help students identify the terminal activity in a center. Most center activities are clearly defined and the activity is ended when the directions are executed. However, a center such as creative writing, (in which students are expected to write about their feelings towards a picture or an incident) may not have a clearly defined point of completion. What are the students to do? Should they place the paper on your desk? Should they hand the paper to you for approval? Should they evaluate their own papers? When the terminal activity is clear to students, they will know when they have completed the activity.

- Let parents know what you are doing with centers. Students often have trouble communicating the nature of center activities to parents. Parents might see them as pure fun and games. A brief note to parents explaining what centers are and how they are being used can save many problems for you. Some teachers have invited parents to school to be present while the center activity is in operation. Others have asked parents to help construct centers. Displaying centers at a parent-teacher meeting is an effective way to help parents understand the nature of center activities. Parents want to know what activities are being conducted in school. Prior information of this nature reduces anxiety and builds support.

Initial Evaluation

Determine a means for evaluating center effectiveness before center use begins. Then, at any time you choose, you can evaluate the worth of a specific learning center. Four questions seem to be of particular worth for this type of evaluation:

1. Are students enjoying the activities?

2. Is classroom behavior satisfactory during center time?

3. Do the centers seem to be fulfilling a needed function (reinforcement, for example)?

4. Are the advantages worth the extra time involved?

After several weeks, an evaluation as simple as this can help you decide if you want to continue with centers. Do not hesitate to ask a colleague to assist you with such an evaluation or ask the students. If conclusions are not certain, continue for a while to see how things work out. Most teachers have found centers to be extremely valuable and worth the effort. However, if, in your case, you find that centers do not meet your instructional needs, discontinue using them for a while and try them again at a later date.

Some Tips to Help Students Use Centers Successfully

Help students understand what they are to do if they:

1. can't read a word necessary to complete work with a center activity,

2. can't complete a given activity,

3. are not interested in a center once they start it,

4. finish a center and have time remaining,

5. haven't time to finish a given center.

Solutions to these problems might be generated through group discussion, and listed for students' reference. From time to time, it would be helpful to review these alternative solutions with students in group or conference situations. Some teachers include this type of information in center directions.

Here are some alternative solutions which one group of students developed for problem number 1 (A student can't read a word necessary to complete work with a center activity.):

1. Try to figure it out.

2. Ask the center helper, see page 51.

3. Ask a friend.

4. Ask the teacher during conference time or at a time set aside for questions.

5. Go on to another activity, and come back to that one when you know the word.

Remember that because centers focus on student self-selection and self-direction, it should not be necessary for all students to have to complete all center activities that they start.

If you are getting started with centers, you may find it helpful to chart your progress on the checklist below.

Check List for Getting Started		
	Yes	No
Have students been well informed concerning the operation of learning centers?		
Have parents been informed about the operation of learning centers?		
Have feedback systems on centers been provided?		
Has provision for an evaluation of each center been made?		
Have rules been established for the use of centers?		
Are students given an opportunity to use meaningful decision-making procedures with centers?		
If students need help, do they know where help might be obtained?		

Chapter 5

Evaluation

How do I evaluate student progress with center activities?
How do I evaluate the effectiveness of my centers?

Evaluation has been discussed in several sections of this book, Chapter 2, page 18; Chapter 3, pages 44 and 51; and Chapter 4, page 54. If you have not looked at those sections, then do so now since this section will not overlap them.

Teachers who are using learning centers should focus on three aspects of evaluation:

The process that a student uses while working in a center.

The product a student develops while working in a center.

The center itself.

Evaluation of Process

Using student self-evaluation, teacher observation, or student-teacher conferences, the teacher should collect data concerning how the student works in a center.

Is the student:

- on task
- interested
- working with care
- enjoying his activity?

Does he:

- work better in some centers than others,
- function better with certain types of activities than with others,
- select activities involving specific learning behaviors,
- work best alone or in a small group,
- finish his work efficiently?

Observing how students work in centers, or the processes they use in working with centers, can give you insight concerning their learning style, their problem-solving strategies, and their ability to work independently. It is useful to keep some records on the processes you observe so you can identify areas of strength and areas of need. It is helpful to compare students' responses to center activities with their responses to teacher directed activities.

Looking at processes will help you in two specific ways. You may decide that certain types of centers are not useful for a given student. If so, that student might best be directed toward other types of centers. Or, you may decide that before working in certain types of centers, some students need specific teacher direction. Only process analysis can give you the data to deal with these aspects of instructional adjustment.

Evaluation of Product

We are all accustomed to evaluating the products of students' work. Product evaluation can be done by the student in a self-correcting manner, by the teacher using either check quizzes or examination of the product, or by student-teacher conferences.

Is the product:

- of sufficient quality
- accurate
- fully completed
- appropriate to the activities of the center?

As a rule, it is probably best not to grade the work done in centers. Unless the work is monitored, you will not really know how much of the work is the responsibility of the student. If you can make comments about the strengths of the student's work and some suggestions about how he might operate the next time, then the evaluation is much more useful.

Again, it is recommended that the evaluation be recorded in some manner. If poor quality products appear consistently, there may be a problem with the centers. Such an observation would lead you to an evaluation of the process or an evaluation of the center itself.

By evaluating products, you can make several decisions. Perhaps the product is not acceptable because the center purpose is unclear. Or perhaps the student is not interested in the activity. Perhaps the student needs preparation prior to working in a given center.

Evaluation of the Center Itself

When you have worked hard to develop effective centers, it is often uncomfortable to evaluate them because you might have to conclude that the center is not effective. However, it is important to look carefully at all the centers which have been constructed. The centers can be evaluated by the teacher, by an individual student, or by a critique group.

Does the center have:

- choices for students
- relevant items included
- clear objectives and purposes
- attractive features
- levels of difficulty
- answers provided?

The effectiveness of a center often can be increased by making small changes such as writing more specific directions. When small changes are made so that students can use center activities successfully, the center becomes a more effective instructional tool.

Students sometimes have reactions to centers which teachers do not anticipate. Student input in evaluation often provides clues as to how centers can be improved. As was suggested previously, students often enjoy helping the teacher modify and improve existing centers, and their advice is usually quite reliable and to the point.

A system for evaluation of an educational activity has been developed by James Raths, of the University of Illinois. Using what he calls a recipe system, he reasons that centers can be evaluated objectively. This is how it works.

List the characteristics that you want to include in most of your centers. For example, you may want most of your centers to contain answers, levels of difficulty, clear directions, and clear purposes. Then, make out a checklist such as the one below. Give the center a number 1 if it has the characteristic you have listed and a 2 if it does not. The evaluation might look like the following:

Learning Centers Evaluation

Learning Center:	A	B	C	D
Levels of difficulty	1	1	2	1
Answers	1	2	2	1
Clear directions	1	1	1	2
Clear purposes	2	2	2	2
Relevant materials	1	2	1	2
Manipulation	1	2	2	1

Data from such an evaluation can be used in several ways. For example, you might decide that center "C" needs major changes to make it useful. You may examine center "A," make the purpose clear, and have a much better center. You might look for more relevant materials to put in centers "B" and "D." You might well decide that there is no way to provide levels of difficulty for center "C."

It is most appropriate for this type of evaluation to be done by the teacher who made the center. Self-evaluation of this type has proven to be very useful. It does not imply right and wrong. It simply provides the teacher with an opportunity to step back and look objectively at what has been done.

By evaluation of process, product, and the centers themselves, the teacher gains insight and can profit from what has been learned. In this way centers will become increasingly effective and learning will become more enjoyable for the students.

Chapter 6

Answers to Questions about Centers

What problems have teachers had in using centers?

Some of My Students Do Not Enjoy Using Learning Centers.

When a student does not enjoy using learning centers, an important first step in helping him develop a more positive attitude toward centers is to ask him why he does not like to use centers. His reply may give you all the information you need. Here are some additional suggestions which may be useful:

- The student may not be interested in the center activities. Identify the interests of the student and build a center which focuses on one of his interests.

- Center activities in your classroom may not be appropriate for the student. Examine the centers which are in use in the classroom. Are they too difficult for the student who does not enjoy using them?

- The student may feel insecure about working independently. Assign a buddy to work with him until he feels more comfortable.

- Provide alternatives for the student who cannot operate successfully with any center activity. Don't force him to work in centers if he feels very negatively about them.

- The student may need more adult attention in the form of teacher directed activities and teacher-student conferences.

All of My Students Want to Work with the Same Center.

Some centers are extremely popular with students. Often these are centers which are colorful, manipulative, related to students'

61

interests, and at an appropriate level of difficulty. Try to determine what characteristics of the center are most appealing to your students, and consider incorporating these characteristics into other centers. Another suggestion which may help you solve this problem is to guide student's use of the center. For example:

- Assign specific students to use the center at specific times.

- Place a limit on the number of students who are to work at that center.

- Develop a sign-up sheet or obtain a sign-up board for use with each center. Indicate on the sheet or board how many students may work with the center.

- Have students contract or negotiate for use of centers.

Some of your centers may be competing with one another for student attention. An activity which involves constructing a model house out of blocks or rolling trucks along a "road" may be competing with activities requiring paper-pencil responses. If you find that you have competing centers, you may wish to use them at different times during the day or week, or follow some of the suggestions for guiding self-selection listed above.

Many of My Center Activities Get Lost or Destroyed.

If loss or destruction of center activities is a major problem for you, it may reflect a general problem of student use of materials or a general problem of classroom organization. Are materials other than center materials consistently lost or destroyed? If the problem seems to be general in nature, a different strategy for classroom management or student supervision may be needed. However, if the problem seems to be specifically related to center activities, consider these alternatives:

- Examine the centers to determine if they are too difficult. Students may be destroying the centers because they feel frustrated with tasks involved in the center activities.

- Get students involved in constructing centers so that they feel a sense of pride and accomplishment toward the centers.

- Assign center helpers to assist you in keeping the center activities from becoming lost or destroyed.

- Make your centers as durable as possible through use of sturdy materials, clear contact paper, lamination, etc.

- Have a "Lost and Found" box for center parts and pieces.

- Include a statement such as this as a final step in developing center directions: "Replace the parts of the center. Be sure everything is here."

- Discuss the problem with students to enlist their suggestions and advice.

- Present centers as a privilege to be given if students demonstrate responsible care and use of the activities.

- Remove centers from the classroom until you feel that you have discussed the problem satisfactorily with students.

- Remember that centers will "wear out" naturally as students use them. The more popular the center, the more likely it is to become worn.

My Students Avoid Certain Centers.

When you find your students avoiding a certain center, it is helpful to ask students to explain why they are avoiding it. You could ask a group of students to critique the center. Their comments may help you analyze the center and make appropriate modifications.

Another strategy which teachers find helpful is to compare the popular centers with those which are avoided. What characteristics do the centers have in common? What are their differences? Centers are sometimes avoided by students for these reasons:

- Too much writing is required.
- Too much copying is required.
- Centers contain busy work.
- Center is unattractive.
- Center is uninteresting.

- Center is too difficult.
- Directions are confusing.

If you can determine why the center is being avoided, you may be able to make it more appealing, see Initial Evaluation, page 54. Students' reactions to centers often provide a very clear indication of the types of modifications which are needed.

My Students Pace Themselves Unwisely When They Are Using Centers.

If you consider self-pacing as a process of pacing yourself to success, several possible solutions to the problem of self-pacing can be offered. Two factors are involved in pacing yourself to success: a factor of time, i.e., how rapidly or how slowly will you work in order to accomplish your objectives, and a factor of selection, i.e., what materials, activities, and assistance -- and what order and combination of these -- will you select in order to successfully accomplish your objectives. When students have problems with pacing, it may be a problem of time or a problem of selection.

Problems of pacing as it relates to time may occur when:
- Students have been assigned too many centers and rush to complete them.
- Students have difficulty determining when a task has been completed and when to move on to another task.
- Students have problems with self-selection.
- Students are unable to set realistic goals for themselves.

Although it is important for students to pace themselves through center activities, they frequently need assistance to determine an appropriate pace. Hold conferences with students who appear to need help with pacing. You might set the pace for a while by giving students suggested time limits for various activities. Or help students to set realistic goals for themselves. If additional assistance appears to be needed, you may want to assign buddies to work with the students or you might ask the students to explain their work to you upon completion.

If selection of materials, activities, and assistance in accomplishing certain objectives seem to be standing in the path of success for some students, consider:

- Assisting them with the process of selection by indicating the activities and materials which may be of most help to them.

- Obtaining diagnostic information on the skill strengths and needs of the students to be certain the centers in the classroom meet their needs.

- Contracting with the students in such a manner that they work with you to determine which centers they will select, and how they will demonstrate what they have accomplished.

- Developing additional centers for these students when needed.

- Making centers multi-level so students can find a point at which to make a successful beginning and so that students can move to an easier or more difficult activity within the center depending upon their needs.

My Students Do Not Take Center Activities Seriously.

If your students do not take center activities seriously, it is important for you to determine how you honestly feel about the centers you are using in the classroom, and how you feel about center use in general. Do you feel that centers should be activities which are available to students only after all other required tasks are completed? If so, your students may feel that you value the other activities more than you value the centers, and they may conclude that centers are less important than other tasks which they are to do. Or, they may feel the centers are another type of "rainy day game" available if they want to use them.

Another explanation for the attitude of your students toward center activities may be that they are not receiving feedback from you concerning their work at centers. Perhaps it would be helpful to schedule individual or small group conferences to discuss activities which students have used in centers.

Examine the activities which are in the centers. Are they worthwhile? Do students understand why the activities are included in the centers? Are the students aware of the purposes and objectives of the center activities? If students feel that the activities are "busy work" for them, or if they cannot see the relationship between center activities and other curriculum activities, they may not take center activities seriously. You might try including the purpose of the center activity in the center directions, or you might discuss its purpose with the students.

The Parents in My School Community Do Not Approve of Centers.

Do the parents in your community understand the purpose of centers? It may be that they do not understand the relationship of centers to the curriculum. Identify a way to explain to parents your rationale for using centers and their relationship to the rest of the curriculum. You may choose to do this at the beginning of the school year through a letter to parents or through a discussion at a parent-teacher association meeting. It may be helpful to enlist your principal's help and support in explaining the rationale for using centers.

Most parents grow enthusiastic about the use of learning centers when they become involved in constructing centers and assist students to use center activities. Here are some tips to get parents involved with centers:

- Invite parents to observe students using centers.
- Have students explain to visiting parents what center activities they are doing and why they are doing the activities.
- Encourage parent volunteers to assist students with some centers. Parents can assist with reading directions, correcting responses, and general management.
- Involve parents as aides in constructing centers. Give parents a "blueprint" to follow which will direct them in constructing centers. Some parents have artistic talent which can be used to make centers attractive and appealing to students.

My School Administration Questions the Use of Learning Centers.

Perhaps the administration questions your use of learning centers because a rationale for the use of centers has not been presented, or because it is unclear how the use of centers will be integrated with the ongoing curriculum. You may wish to include some of the information from Chapter One in discussing with the administration your rationale for using centers. It is especially helpful to emphasize these points:

- Centers help a teacher individualize an instructional program in situations where students have wide ranges of abilities.
- Centers can be used to meet specific needs of individual students.
- Centers help students direct their own learning, and grow toward independence.

Center Construction Takes Too Much Time.

More teacher time is involved when centers are used, but there are many suggestions you might follow in order to make more efficient use of the time you spend planning and constructing centers. Many suggestions are offered in Chapter 2, Developing Centers, see page 26. The tips summarized below will help you get started.

- Recruit parent volunteers to assist you with construction. With appropriate guidance, their help can be invaluable.
- Plan ways in which students can assist with construction.
- Plan centers in which the same "backdrop" is used, but specific tasks within the center are changed.
- Send a list of needed supplies to parents and community businesses to obtain a supply of materials such as cans, boxes, bags, wallpaper scraps, cardboard, contact paper, posters, window decorations, etc.
- Use very sturdy materials so centers are durable.
- Share centers with other teachers.

I Don't Know What to Do About Grading the Work Which Students Do in Centers.

You may wish to distinguish between grading tasks which students do in centers, and grading the overall development of a skill or accomplishment of objectives. For example, specific center activities might not need to be graded. Instead, students would receive a grade for the accomplishment of specific skills or objectives as measured by their performance on a post test. The center would be a learning activity and not a testing activity. The test would be developed to assess the accomplishment of objectives specified by the center and related teacher directed activities.

As you attempt to answer the question of grading students for work done in centers, consider these suggestions:

- Keep records of center activities which students have used, and the types of responses they have made to these activities.
- Use students' performances with center activities in conjunction with other data.
- Use mastery tests to grade students instead of grading their center work.
- Set standards in advance and expect quality work in centers, but do not confuse learning and testing situations.
- Include post tests in some centers -- if appropriate -- as last steps.
- In some centers, consider having as a last step a project to be submitted for a grade.

My Students Look at Answers Before They Attempt to Do the Activity.

Remember that learning centers are designed for independent student learning -- not testing. Looking at answers may greatly assist some students with the learning involved in specific centers. By looking at an answer, a student may get the clue he needs to comprehend a task or skill. However, if you feel that students are looking at answers too frequently, here are some suggestions you can try.

- Make answer keys which you keep in a separate answer file. Completion of a task can be the prerequisite for consulting the answer keys.
- Use teacher correction instead of student correction of answers.
- Tell students to let you know when they are able to accomplish tasks in center activities without first looking at the answers.
- Examine centers to determine if they are too difficult for students.
- Encourage students to work with a partner to solve difficult tasks.

Chapter 7

Idea Bank

The Idea Bank is divided into sections with each section focusing on ideas related to a specific curriculum area. Several ideas for basic center activities are included.

Each idea is described in a format that includes this information:

- an illustration of the basic center activity,
- the curriculum area for which it was designed,
- the purpose of the center activity,
- the specific objectives around which the center activity was planned,
- the materials needed to construct the activity,
- the directions for using the center activity, and
- the feedback or evaluation procedure used with the center activity.

It is most important to note that these basic center activities do not represent fully developed centers. Rather, each basic activity is intended to be used as an **idea starter** for teachers to extend, modify, and/or adapt to fit their individual teaching situations.

The Idea Bank will be most helpful when it is viewed as a reference presenting **idea starters** with extensive suggestions for individualizing the activities to fit specific teaching situations.

Each basic center activity is followed by these types of suggestions:

1. How to extend the basic activity with related activities which are easier, related activities which are more difficult, and related activities which are open-ended.

2. How to modify specific characteristics of the center activities such as their manipulative features, the techniques used for self-correction, and the types of directions which are included.

3. How to adapt the format of the basic center idea to content from other curriculum areas.

Here are some important points to consider if you are selecting one of these basic center ideas to extend, modify, or adapt.

1. Identify objectives which are appropriate for your students and your curriculum. If the objectives presented with the center activities in the Idea Bank do not appear to be appropriate for your situation, modify the activities to coincide with your objectives. Be sure to include a statement of the center objectives on the center which you develop. (See Chapter 2, p. 6 for information related to identifying and writing objectives.)

2. Decide how many activities to include in your center. Should these activities be more simple, more complex, or more open-ended than the basic idea presented in the Idea Bank? (For additional ideas on making centers multi-level, refer to Chapter 2, p.14 .)

3. Consider the ability of your students to read directions. Can they read the directions included with the basic idea in the Idea Bank, or will the directions need to be modified? (Chapter 2, p. 23 reviews ways to present center directions.)

4. Assimilate use of the center into your strategy for center organization and management. The basic center ideas described in the Idea Bank do not include information concerning important details of organization and management, i.e., record-keeping procedures, number of students who can work at the center, since these details are unique to each teaching situation. (Chapter 3 discusses information concerning organization and management in depth.)

I. Basic Center Idea

Area: Reading

Purpose: To reinforce phonics skills through initial consonant
              substitution.

Objectives: Students will read words made by adding initial conson-
              ants to 'it,' 'at,' and 'in.' Students will use the words in
              sentences.

Materials: Train cars made from construction paper or boxes
              Letter cards
              Tape with answers
              Tape recorder.

Directions: 1. Work with one car at a time. Read the word on the car.
              2. Take the letter cards out of the car.
              3. Put each letter card at the beginning of the word on
                 the car to make a new word.
              4. Read the word you have made.
              5. Use it in a sentence.
              6. Check your work by listening to the words on the tape
                 when you have finished.

Evaluation: Self-check: Listen to answers on tape, e.g., "When you
              add 's' to 'it' you make the word sit. You can sit in a
              chair."

II. How to Extend the Basic Center Idea

A. To make the activity easier

1. Use fewer initial consonants in each "train."
2. Put directions on tape so that the word is read to the student. The student makes the word that he hears on the tape, and then reads the word himself, e.g., "Add 't' to 'in' and you have 'tin.' Make the word 'tin' now by adding 't' to 'in'."
3. Give picture clues on the initial consonant cards.
4. Work with a partner.

B. To make the activity more difficult

1. Use more difficult word endings such as -ought, -ight.
2. Use consonant blends instead of single consonants.
3. Substitute final consonants instead of initial consonants.
4. Substitute medial vowels instead of initial consonants.
5. Put the words in a story context.
   John will _et the new dog for his birthday. He will _et the dog's dish in the house so it will not get _et if it rains.
6. Have students write the words in sentences after they have done the initial consonant substitution.
7. Have students choose an appropriate word to fit a sentence.
   Lisa and Mike will_____ new bikes.

   set   get   wet

C. To make the activity open-ended

1. Have students make their own "consonant trains" and give them to a friend to use.
2. Have students collect or create pictures of objects suitable for inclusion in cars of the consonant train you have made.

III. How to Modify the Basic Center Idea

A. Other ways to make the center activity manipulative

1. Use train puzzles.
2. Use a pocket chart with letter and word cards.
3. Use word strips with slots to insert letters.
4. Use a series of tachistoscopes.

B. Other ways to provide feedback about the activity

1. Use a mastery test after students have done all activities within the center.
2. Use the pupil response cards for small group teacher directed activities. For example, the teacher holds up the word 'in' and

asks students to hold up the letter card needed to make the word 'tin.'

   3. Have a center helper read the words to the student when the student has finished.

C. Other ways to prepare directions for the center

   1. Tape directions.

   2. Use diagrams or photos.

IV. How to Adapt the Basic Center Idea to Other Curriculum Areas

A. Reading/Language Arts: Place a prefix or suffix on each card in the train. Each train might have a root word written on it. Students would add prefixes and/or suffixes to the word on the train to make a new word. Words should be used in sentences.

B. Math: Place a number on each card in every train, and another number on each train. Numbers on the train might be added to, subtracted from, multiplied by, or divided by the number on the card in the train.

C. Health: Label each train with the name of one of the food groups. Pictures of food could be located in a separate box. Students could put the pictures in the appropriate train car.

D. Social Studies: Label train cars with the names of places (counties, states, countries -- depending on the area of study and age of students). Names of specific places within the areas designated on the cars might be placed in a separate box. Students would put the specific places in the appropriate train car.

I. Basic Center Idea

Area: Reading

Purpose: To reinforce vocabulary through use of word opposites.

Objective: Students will identify word opposites.

Materials: Cardboard circle or paper plate
            Wooden clothespins (snap type)
            Sets of word opposites
            Magic marker.

Directions: 1. Read the words on the plate.
            2. Read the words on the pins. Match the opposites.
            3. Check by looking on the back.

Evaluation: Self-check: Answers are on the back of the plate.

II. How to Extend the Basic Center Idea

A. To make the activity easier

  1. Use pictures on the plate and on the pins.
  2. Use pictures on the plate and words on the pins.
  3. Use fewer words.
  4. Use easier words.

B. To make the activity more difficult

1. Use more words.
2. Use more difficult words.
3. Include extra pins containing word distractors, e.g., ten word pins, eight words on the plate.
4. Use the words in a sentence context.

C. To make the idea open-ended

1. Have students construct the activity using words of their choice.
2. Have students create illustrations to go with pairs of word opposites.

III. How to Modify the Basic Center Idea

A. Other ways to make the center activity manipulative

1. Put the pairs of word opposites on puzzles.
2. Put the pairs of word opposites on pocket cards.
3. Use sets of picture or word cards on a flannel board.
4. Make a matching activity using yarn or shoestrings.
5. Use a worksheet containing words in context.

B. Other ways to provide feedback about the activity

1. Prepare a separate answer key.

C. Other ways to prepare directions for the center

1. Put the directions on tape.
2. Write the directions on a separate card or chart.

IV. How to Adapt the Basic Center Idea to Other Curriculum Areas

A. Reading/Language Arts: Construct matching activities such as the following: match contractions, match compound words, match synonyms, match words to complete analogies, match parts of speech with words.

B. Math: Develop matching activities such as: match number facts with answers, match numerals with sets, match problems with answers, match numbers with different bases.

C. Science: Use matching activities such as the following: match inventions with inventors, match animals with classification categories, match simple machines with examples of the machines.

D. Social Studies: Prepare matching activities such as these: match picture with person from the news, match state with capital, match city with state, match explorer with territory discovered.

I. Basic Center Idea

Area: Reading

Purpose: To reinforce comprehension skills in the area of main idea.

Objective: Students will identify from a group of sentences those which go with a picture and those which do not.

Materials: A large picture of high interest to students
Strips containing sentences
Box appropriately labeled to hold sentence strips
"Yes" pocket
"No" pocket.

Directions: 1. Take a card from the box.
2. Read the sentences on the cards.
3. Study the picture and decide if the sentence goes with it.
4. Put sentences that go with the picture in the "Yes" pocket. Put sentences that do not go with the picture in the "No" pocket.
5. Check your work by turning over each card.
6. Put the sentence cards back in the box.

Evaluation: Self-check: Answers are on the back of the card.

II. How to Extend the Basic Center Idea

A. To make the activity easier

1. Use a picture with few details.
2. Use a picture illustrating an activity within the experiential background of the students.
3. Write sentences that can be answered from the specific information given in the picture.
4. Use words instead of sentences in a type of labeling activity.
5. Tape the sentences instead of writing them. Students check "Yes" or "No" on a response sheet as they listen to each sentence.

B. To make the activity more difficult

1. Use a picture with many details.
2. Use a picture illustrating an activity outside the experiential background of the students.
3. Use a map or diagram.
4. Write sentences that require critical or creative thinking rather than simply locating information, e.g., "This may be the beginning of a moon mission."
5. Relate the activity to distinguishing fact from opinion.
6. Include more difficult vocabulary in the sentences.
7. Use more than one picture and have students match sentences to the appropriate pictures. Include some distractors among the sentences.
8. Use paragraphs rather than sentences.

C. To make the activity open-ended

1. Have students write sentences to go with a specific picture.

2. Have students write sentences to go with pictures they have selected. (Students might include distractors among sentences they write.)
3. Have students select advertisements from magazines, cut the captions from the ads, and give them to a friend to match.

III. How to Modify the Basic Center Idea

A. Other ways to make the center activity manipulative

1. List sentences on a chart beside the picture. Students place a "Yes" card beside all sentences that go with the picture.
2. List the sentences on a ditto sheet. Students check the sentences that go with the picture.
3. Use small pictures and write sentences on small cards. Use in a pocket chart, or in a folder.

B. Other ways to provide feedback about the activity

1. Use a separate answer key.
2. Use a color code or a number code.

C. Other ways to prepare directions for the center

1. Put directions on tape.

IV. How to Adapt the Basic Center Idea to Other Curriculum Areas

A. Reading/Language Arts: Have students write sentences describing a high interest picture using words from their spelling lists. Students might write descriptive paragraphs about the picture.

B. Math: Use graphs instead of pictures. Write sentences which relate to interpretation of the graph.
Use an ad from a newspaper which lists prices of items. Write sentences such as, "The 28-inch bike is less expensive than the 29-inch bike." If the statement goes with the ad, it is placed in the "Yes" pocket.

C. Science: Use a picture illustrating a science concept. Sentences could contain science related statements.

D. Social Studies: Use a political cartoon, a map, or newspaper photo in place of the picture. Sentences could be newspaper headlines.

Idea adapted from a center developed by Linda Miller, Howard County, Maryland.

I. Basic Center Idea

Area: Reading

Purpose: To reinforce comprehension skills in the area of distinguishing facts from opinions.

Objectives: Students will identify statements of fact and statements of opinion.

Materials: Index cards
Cans or boxes labeled "F" and "O"
Envelopes for cards

Directions: 1. Read the statement on each card.
          2. Put the cards that present a statement of fact in the "F" can. Put the cards that present a statement of opinion in the "O" can.
          3. Check your work by looking on the back of the card.

Evaluation: Self-check: Answers are on the back of the cards.

II. How to Extend the Basic Center Idea

A. To make the activity easier

  1. Present a statement of fact and a statement of opinion on each card, both related to the same topic, e.g., "Dogs are canines. Dogs are warm, friendly pets." Have students indicate which is a statement of fact and which is a statement of opinion.

  2. Present one statement of fact and one statement of opinion related to a picture of interest to students. (Students identify the statement of opinion.)

B. To make the activity more difficult

1. Have students locate statements of fact and statements of opinion in newspapers and magazines.
2. Present ten statements of fact. Have students write a statement of opinion connected with each statement of fact.

C. To make the activity open-ended

1. Have students write ten statements of fact and ten statements of opinion, and prepare a separate answer key. These statements can be given to a friend to do.
2. Have students analyze advertisements to locate statements of fact and statements of opinion in the ads.

III. How to Modify the Basic Center Idea

A. Other ways to make the center manipulative

1. Use an electric board with statements on one side and "F" and "O" on the other.
2. Write each statement on a pocket card and attach it to the bulletin board. Have students insert tab cards into the pocket cards.

B. Other ways to provide feedback about the activity

1. Use a separate answer key on which each statement is listed and coded.
2. Number each card. Place the numbers of the cards belonging in each can or box on the bottom of the can or box.

C. Other ways to prepare directions for the center

1. Include examples.
2. Include definition of fact and opinion.

IV. How to Adapt the Basic Center Idea to Other Curriculum Areas

A. Reading/Language Arts: Write declarative and interrogative sentences on the cards omitting punctuation. Label cans with appropriate punctuation marks.

B. Math: Write word problems on cards. Label cans with the process symbols of +, −, x and ÷. Students place the problem card in the can indicating the process used to solve the problem.

C. Science: Place pictures on cards. Label cans "animal," "vegetable," and "mineral." Students place picture cards in the appropriate can.

D. Social Studies: Write names of cities, states, and countries on the cards. Label cans accordingly.

I. Basic Center Idea

Area: Reading

Purpose: To reinforce comprehension skills in the area of critical reading.

Objective: Students will identify "gimmicks" and descriptive adjectives (advertising techniques) designed to persuade the consumer.

Materials: Large collection of flattened commercial packages
Large cardboard box to contain packages
Several smaller appropriately labeled boxes
Magic marker   Pencil
Paper   Glue.

Directions: The packages in the large box are printed with advertising "gimmicks" and descriptive adjectives.
1. Read each package and list on your paper all adjectives which reflect the advertiser's opinion of the product.
2. Compare your answers to those written on the back of the large box which contains the packages.
3. Place each package in the box which best describes the type of "gimmick" found on the package.
4. Compare your answers to those written on the lids of the smaller boxes.

Evaluation: Self-check: Step one answers are listed on the back of the large box.
Step three answers appear on the lids of the smaller boxes.

II. How to Extend the Basic Center Idea

A. To make the activity easier

1. Limit the quantity of commercial packages.
2. Limit the kind of commercial packages, e.g., food products only.
3. Limit activity to step one only.
4. Limit activity to step three only.
5. Identify only one "gimmick" on a variety of packages.

B. To make the activity more difficult

1. Match the type of "gimmick" with the type of person to whom it is meant to appeal, e.g., comics to children, recipes to mother.
2. Include a search for additives on food products.
3. Include a search for warnings and cautions on household products.

C. To make the activity open-ended

1. Direct students to design their own commercial package using descriptive adjectives, "gimmicks," cautions, etc..
2. Have students collect examples of advertising techniques on commercial packages.

III. How to Modify the Basic Center Idea

A. Other ways to make the center manipulative

1. Place packages on a bulletin board. Use color coded pins and a key to identify categories, e.g., red pins - descriptive adjectives. Students place the pins directly on the packages.

2. Laminate packages and have students mark their responses directly on the packages using a grease pencil, e.g., circle descriptive adjectives.
3. Place packages in a box or on a bulletin board or in a folder and have responses recorded on a worksheet.

B. Other ways to provide feedback about the activity

1. Prepare a tape with answers and explanations.
2. Prepare a separate answer sheet and keep it in a folder.
3. Place answers on a bulletin board, in a file box or on the back of each package.

C. Other ways to prepare directions for the center

1. Put directions as well as corrections on tape. Include a brief explanation of advertising techniques designed to persuade the consumer.
2. Write directions on a worksheet.
3. Place directions in a file box or a folder.

IV. How to Adapt the Basic Center Idea to Other Curriculum Areas

A. Math: Compare price of package to quantity of the product. For example, compute the unit price for three or four brands of the same product.

B. Science: Have students search for harmful chemicals in products and discriminate between natural ingredients and synthetics in those products.

C. Health: Have students classify food products into food groups. Students might make recipes found on commercial packages or develop recipes based on the commercial products.

D. Social Studies: Relate the activity to a unit on "The Consumer." For example, have students plan advertising campaigns for real or imaginary products to appeal to specific sections of the consumer market.

Idea adapted from a center developed by Ellen Hormanski, Howard County, Maryland.

PLACE THE ROCKET WITH YOUR NAME BESIDE THE STAR
WHICH DESCRIBES WHAT YOU ARE MAKING.

I. Basic Center Idea

Area: Reading

Purpose: To reinforce comprehension skills in the area of following directions.

Objective: The student will follow written directions by constructing items for which written directions are given. (Written directions are for making or doing specific things, e.g., popping popcorn, paper-folding, performing simple science experiments, and following directions on a map.)

Materials:

Magic marker	Paper
Scissors	Map
Science materials	Popcorn equipment.

Directions: These directions are given orally to the group.

1. Choose the activity you prefer and read the directions carefully.
2. Do all the steps in the activity.
3. Check your answers or show your completed project to the teacher.
4. Choose two more activities which interest you.

5. Complete the activities.
6. Check your work by comparing your project with the model.

Evaluation: Self-check: Models of the completed items are located in a separate packet.

II. How to Extend the Basic Center Idea

A. To make the activity easier

1. Have students construct items having fewer steps.
2. Have students construct items with simpler directions.
3. Have models available for student reference throughout their work on the projects.
4. Illustrate each step in the directions.
5. Have students work in teams.

B. To make the activity more difficult

1. Include items with many steps.
2. Include items with challenging directions.
3. Have students write directions for a specific task or item.
4. Describe or display an item which is incorrectly constructed or completed. Have students identify which parts of the directions for making the item were not followed correctly.

C. To make the activity open-ended

1. Have students select an item for which they prepare directions, e.g., how to prepare a favorite food; how to build a model airplane.
2. Have students collect examples of directions which they feel are unclear, and rewrite those directions.
3. Have students teach other students or a group of students to construct something.

III. How to Modify the Basic Center Idea

A. Other ways to make the center manipulative

1. Use a game board on which students move from space to space as they complete parts of directions which have been presented.
2. Laminate parts of center activities so students can write or draw on them.

B. Other ways to provide feedback about the activity

   1. Have peers who have successfully completed activities assist students with self-checking.

C. Other ways to prepare directions for the center

   1. Put directions on tape.
   2. Prepare a set of photos illustrating step-by-step procedures to follow.
   3. Have peers who have successfully completed the activity explain it to others.

IV. How to Adapt the Basic Center Idea to Other Curriculum Areas

A. Math: Have students construct geometric figures; have students construct items in which mathematical computations must be used in measuring items used in construction; or have students construct charts and graphs.

B. Science: Have students construct scientific models by following directions; or have students conduct experiments using step-by-step directions.

C. Social Studies: Have students construct models of communities, relief maps, time lines, etc. following specific directions.

Idea adapted from a center developed by Gail Brotman, Howard County, Maryland.

I. Basic Center Idea

Area: Language Arts

Purpose: To reinforce alphabetizing skills.

Objectives: Students will put letters in alphabetical order. Students will put words in alphabetical order.

Materials: Letter cards   Word cards
Red pockets   Blue pockets.
Magic marker or pen

Directions: Part A
1. Work with one red pocket at a time. There are six letters in each pocket.
2. Put the letters in A-B-C order.
3. Check your answers by looking at the numbers on the back of the cards.
4. Try another pocket.

Part B
1. Work with one blue pocket at a time. There are six words in each pocket.
2. Put the words in A-B-C order.

3. Check your answers by looking at the numbers on the back of the cards.
4. Try another pocket.

Evaluation: Self-check: Alphabetical order is shown by a numeral on the back of each card.

II. How to Extend the Basic Center Idea

A. To make the activity easier

1. Prepare a set of letter strips. On each strip write three letters and include one blank space. Prepare a separate set of small letter cards. On each card write one of the letters which could be used to fill in the blank spaces on the letter strips. Students place the appropriate letter on each blank space.
2. Place an alphabet strip on the front of each letter or word pocket. Students refer to the alphabet strip as needed.
3. Include three (rather than six) letter or word cards in each pocket.

B. To make the activity more difficult

1. Include all 26 letters in a letter pocket. Have students put them in A-B-C order.
2. Use words with the same first letter in one pocket. In another pocket use words with the same first two letters. In a third pocket use words with the same first three letters.

C. To make the activity open-ended

1. Have students develop sets of word cards for peers to place in A-B-C order. Students should include an answer key with their word cards.
2. Have students cut six words beginning with a specific letter (or set of letters) from school newspapers or children's magazines. Students arrange the words in alphabetical order and paste them on a card.
3. Prepare a word game containing a set of twenty to thirty word cards. Students play with one to three partners. One student deals an equal number of cards to each player. Each student places his words in alphabetical order. The first student to complete the activity successfully, is the winner. (Letter cards can be used.)
4. Use the word cards, have groups of students build a word list in alphabetical order.

III. How to Modify the Basic Center Idea

A. Other ways to make the center manipulative

1. Use a puzzle format for letters and words.
2. Have students arrange letter or word cards on a large pocket chart, or on small hooks attached to a bulletin board.
3. Paste small magnets or strips of flannel on the backs of the cards. Students arrange cards on magnetic or flannel boards.

B. Other ways to provide feedback about the activity

1. Use a separate answer key.
2. Paste a picture on the back of a set of letters or words, then cut the letters or words into strips. When letters or words are correctly assembled, the picture will be formed on the back of the card.

C. Other ways to prepare directions for the center

1. Display an example of a completed activity on the chart where directions are displayed.
2. Prepare directions on a ditto sheet in checklist form. Students check off each activity as it is completed.

IV. How to Adapt the Basic Center Idea to Other Curriculum Areas

A. Math: Have students place number cards in order. Sets of cards could be prepared for whole numbers, fractions, decimals, percentages, etc. Problem cards, e.g., $2 + 3 = \_$, could be used in place of number cards. Students could order cards according to answers to problems.

B. Science: Use strips of cards containing information to be ordered. For example, the steps in a simple science experiment, the steps in a cycle, such as, water cycle or life cycle.

C. Social Studies: Use words from Social Studies units in alphabetizing activities. For example, names of states or cities, names of presidents or other historical figures could be used.

Idea adapted from a center developed by Joseph Czarnecki, Anne Arundel County, Maryland and Linda Miller, Howard County, Maryland.

I. Basic Center Idea

Area: Math

Purpose: To reinforce students ability to solve word problems.

Objectives: Students will write and solve equations for word problems.

Materials: Cardboard fish tank
Paper fishes on which word problems are written
Paper clip for each fish
Fishing poles with magnets
Paper
Pencil.

Directions: 1. Use a fishing pole to catch a fish.
2. Read the problem on the fish.
3. Write the equation.
4. Check your answer on the back of the fish.

Evaluation: Self-check: Answers are on the back of the fishes.

II. How to Extend the Basic Center Idea

A. To make the activity easier

1. Use simple equations with numerals containing only one digit.
2. Use only addition equations.

3. Use only subtraction equations.
4. Use rebus problems instead of word problems.
5. Supply counters or rods for students to use in solving the equations.

B. To make the activity more difficult

1. Use more difficult equations.
2. Use more difficult problems requiring more than one operation to solve the problem.
3. Code the fishes and add a "fish-stew" problem. As an example, students would add the answer from the fish with the star code to the answer from the fish with the square code.

C. To make the idea open-ended

1. Have the students create problems for others to solve.
2. Write an equation and have the students write and/or illustrate an appropriate word problem to go with the equation.

III. How to Modify the Basic Center Idea

A. Other ways to make the center activity manipulative

1. Prepare a matching activity in which students match sets of problem cards with corresponding equation cards.
2. Prepare an activity on a large gameboard with a word problem written in each square on the gameboard. To advance from square to square students must write and solve equations for each problem.

B. Other ways to provide feedback about the activity

1. Code the fishes. Place the corresponding codes on the answer cards.
2. Provide matrices.

C. Other ways to prepare directions for the center

1. Place directions on tape.
2. Write directions on individual fish.

IV. How to Adapt the Basic Center Idea to Other Curriculum Areas

A. Reading/Language Arts: Use rebus sentences on the fishes for spelling activities. Students spell the pictured words.

Write words on paper fishes. Students give a word opposite for each word they get when they go fishing.

Use story-starters on fishes. Students write or tape a story to go with the story-starter.

B. Science: Write true-false statements on paper fishes related to a specific science unit. Students go fishing, read the statement, and tell if it is true or false. An example might be, "bricks float."

C. Social Studies: Use as a review activity for a social studies unit. Write the names of people, places and/or events on the fishes. Students go fishing and tell something about the person, place, or event on their fish.

Idea adapted from a center developed by Cecilia Powers Wright, Delaware County, Pennsylvania.

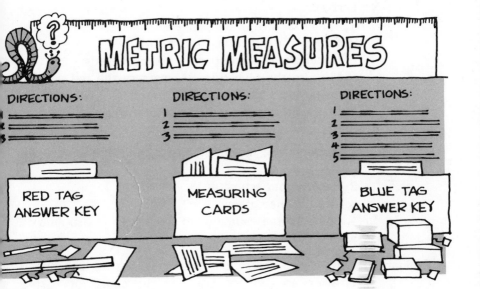

I. Basic Center Idea

Area: Math

Purpose: To reinforce concepts and skills related to metric linear measurement.

Objective: Students will be able to use metric linear measurement (millimeter, centimeter, decimeter, and meter).

Materials: Items to measure labeled with red tags (centimeter and meter), such as, pencils, sheets of paper, etc.

Items to measure labeled with blue tags (millimeter, centimeter, decimeter, meter), such as, shoe laces, erasers, etc.

Cards of various sizes containing directions (millimeter, centimeter, decimeter)

(Each of the four sides to be a different length. Color each edge to be measured a different color.)

Pocket	Meter stick
30 Centimeter stick	Magic marker
Red answer key	Paper
Blue answer key	Pencil.

Directions: Part 1

1. Measure the items with a red tag in centimeters or meters.
2. Record your findings.
3. Check the red answer key.

Part 2
1. Take a card from the pocket.
2. Follow the directions on the card.
   (Examples of directions for different cards:
   Measure the blue side; or, measure the red side; or,
   measure the blue and red side, etc.)
3. Check the answer on the back of the card.

Part 3
1. Estimate the measurements of the items with a blue
   tag.
2. Record your estimates.
3. Measure these items.
4. Compare the estimates to the actual measurements.
5. Check the blue answer key.

Evaluation: Self-check: Separate answer keys for Parts 1 and 3,
answers are on the back of the cards for Part 2.

II. How to Extend the Basic Center Idea

A. To make the activity easier

1. Prepare a bulletin board or large chart which presents metric linear terminology with explanations of each term and examples of
   how each is used. Students can use this chart or bulletin board as
   a reference at any time.
2. Limit the center to centimeter and meter measuring activities.
3. Give the directions in the form of a rebus.
4. Use items which require exact units of one measure.

B. To make the activity more difficult

1. Include terminology and activities pertaining to measurement of
   weight and/or volume.
2. Select a series of objects. Children indicate the most appropriate
   unit of measure for each object. For example, "Would you
   record the length of a room in meters, centimeters, or a combination of both?"
3. Have students answer questions on the basis of their measurement. For example, "Which pencil is longer? How much longer?"
   Then have students answer questions such as "Which is longer, 3
   decimeters or 25 centimeters?"

C. To make the activity open-ended

1. Divide a group of students into two teams.

Team 1	Team 2
1. List objects.	1. Estimate measurements of each object on list.
2. Record measurements of objects separately.	2. Record estimates.
3. Give list to team 2.	3. Measure each object.
	4. Record exact measurements.

Compare estimates to exact measurements and discuss. The teams would alternate procedures. Students should be encouraged to continue to refine their estimating skills. "Bonus Points" could be given for the closest estimates.

2. Prepare a Metric Height Chart. Let students measure each other periodically and record their findings.

III. How to Modify the Basic Center Idea

A. Other ways to make the center activity manipulative

1. Have students use a large pocket chart to categorize metric terminology.
2. Use additional objects for measurement activities.

B. Other ways to provide feedback about the activity

1. Have students bring record sheets to small group sessions for discussion.
2. Record answers on tape with appropriate explanations.

C. Other ways to prepare directions for the activity

1. Discuss directions with students as part of teacher directed activities.
2. Record step-by-step directions on tape.

IV. How to Adapt the Basic Center Idea to Other Curriculum Areas

A. Reading/Language Arts: Prepare several "Recipe Cards." Each card would have a list of directions for drawing a "Metric Creature." For example:

1. Draw a head 5 centimeters square.
2. Draw the body 2 decimeters long.
3. Draw the legs 12 centimeters long.

The children can create additional "Recipe Cards" for others to follow.

B. Science: Give the students a variety of word problems to solve. These problems could be based on your science curriculum, using the metric system. For example, describe a quantity of water needed for a science experiment. "One liter of water is needed, should it be placed in a glass, a jar, or a larger container?"

C. Social Studies: Use metric linear measurement to plan and construct a model of a building, street, city, etc., relevant to a social studies unit.

Idea adapted from a center developed by Dianne Yeager, Chester County, Pennsylvania.

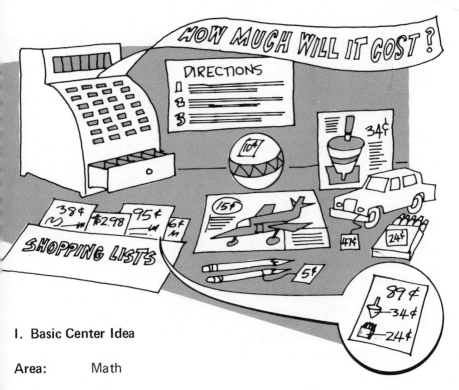

I. Basic Center Idea

Area: Math

Purpose: To reinforce the process of adding and subtracting money.

Objective: The student will make change through adding and subtracting money.

Materials: Cards (containing the amount to be spent and the items to be bought)
Pictures (containing items from catalogues or newspapers)
Shopping list pocket   Magic marker
Glue   Scissors.

Directions: 1. Choose a card. It will tell you how much you have to spend. The card will tell you what you are going to buy.
2. Add the cost of the items.
3. Subtract the cost from the money you have to spend.

Evaluation: Self-check: Answer appears on the reverse side of the card.

II. How to Extend the Basic Center Idea

A. To make the activity easier

1. Have the students use play money to add the cost of the items and to make change.
2. Price the items so that regrouping is not required.
3. Have the students purchase fewer items.

B. To make the activity more difficult

1. Use larger sums of money to purchase more items.
2. Let the students select items from catalogues and newspapers with different spending limits. For example, "Today you have $3.00 to spend at the Hardware Store."
3. List alternative prices for several different items, e.g., potato chips - 15 cents, 25 cents and 39 cents; crayons - 12 cents, 29 cents and 50 cents, etc. The students are to purchase as many items as they can with a specific amount of money.

C. To make the idea open-ended

1. Let the students design and illustrate a catalogue for others to use.
2. Use newspapers and catalogues to make different shopping lists.

III. How to Modify the Basic Center Idea

A. Other ways to make the center activity manipulative

1. Use play money for the students to add the cost of their purchases.
2. Use play money for the students to count change for each item purchased.
3. Have the students plan, build, stock, and price the items in a play store.

B. Other ways to provide feedback about the activity

1. Work in pairs to add the cost of the item and make the correct change.
2. Prepare a mastery test after the students have completed the center activities.

C. Other ways to prepare directions for the center

1. Put the directions on tape.
2. Give the directions in the form of a rebus.

IV. How to Adapt the Basic Center Idea to Other Curriculum Areas

A. Reading/Language Arts: Have students write ads for items to be "sold" in a classroom store. Present ads in a newspaper or poster format. Have students include sale items. For example, ring was 75 cents, now on sale for 50 cents, save 25 cents.

B. Science: Have students find the cost of various foods for school pets, home pets or pets they would like to own. Students could discover how much it would cost to feed a specific pet for a week, two weeks, etc.

C. Social Studies: Select items, pictures, and catalogues related to specific social studies units. For example, set up an Indian Trading Post, a Santa's Toy Shop, a Community Grocery Store or a Rural General Store.

Idea adapted from a center developed by Dianne Yeager, Chester County, Pennsylvania.

I. Basic Center Idea

Area: Science

Purpose: To introduce a health unit on the five senses.

Objective: Students will identify a set of specific items through using one of the five senses: hearing, touching, smelling, looking, and tasting.

Materials: Several numbered jars appropriately labeled containing substances for students to taste, e.g., salt, sugar, etc.
Wooden ice cream spoons for tasting (to be discarded after use)
Large box with a hole covered by a flap of cloth
Several items within the box to be identified by touch, e.g., ball, pencil, etc.
Tape on which several sounds have been recorded, e,g., barking dog, electric mixer, etc.
Several numbered jars appropriately labeled containing substances for students to smell, e.g., cinnamon, pepper, etc.
Several pictures containing hidden objects.
CAUTION: Care should be taken in selecting substances which are not harmful in case students' inappropriately place them in their mouths.

Directions: Part 1
1. Work with a partner.
2. Open one jar at a time.
3. Use a wooden spoon to get something to taste out of the jar.
4. Taste it. What is it? Tell your partner.
5. Check your answer by looking at the answer key.
6. Leave the jars as you found them.

Part 2
1. Put your hand under the flap in the box.
2. Feel each thing inside the box.
3. What do you feel? Draw a picture of each thing you think you felt.
4. Look inside. Were you right?

Part 3
1. Work with a partner.
2. Open one jar at a time.
3. Smell what is inside.
4. Tell your partner what you think is inside.
5. Check your answers by looking at the answer key when you are finished.
6. Leave the jars as you found them.

Part 4
1. Listen to Side 1 of the tape.
2. What do you hear? Draw a picture of each thing you heard.
3. Listen to the answers on Side II. Were you right?

Part 5
1. Look at the pictures.
2. Find the hidden objects in the pictures.
3. Check your work by looking at the answer key.

Evaluation: Self-check: Has been included in each set of directions described above.

II. How to Extend the Basic Center Idea

A. To make the activity easier

1. Select items which are within the everyday experience of the students.

2. Prepare a chart of pictures illustrating all the items within the box, another listing all items to be smelled, another listing or illustrating the source of sounds which appear on the tape, etc. Students first look at the pictures, then identify the specific items following the directions above.

3. Group items for any one task which are easily distinguished, e.g., a barking dog and an electric mixer are more easily distinguished than an electric blender and an electric mixer.

4. Prepare a set of cards for each activity listing the items. Students follow directions above, but match the name of the item with the item.

B. To make the activity more difficult

1. Use items which are similar in taste, smell, texture, sound, etc., so that finer discrimination is needed to identify them.

2. Include some items with which students have had limited experience.

3. Increase the number of items in each activity.

4. Have students categorize items after they have identified them, for example, sounds made by animals as compared to sounds made by motors. Items could be categorized by color, texture, odor, etc.

C. How to make the activity open-ended

1. Have students prepare tapes on which they record common sounds, or "Mystery Boxes" in which they place items for class-mates to feel. Students should prepare an answer key to go with each activity they make.

2. Have students respond to questions after identifying various items. Questions could include:
   a. What other things feel like _____ ?
   b. What other things sound like _____ ?
   c. What other things taste like _____ ?

III. How to Modify the Basic Center Idea

A. Other ways to make the center activity manipulative

1. Use a puzzle format. Place a sample or picture on one half of the card. Write the name on the other half. If the two halves match, the association is correct.

2. Place items to be felt in a solid draw string pouch.

B. Other ways to provide feedback about the activity

1. Have each student work with a partner who has previously worked through the center activities. The partner provides feedback.
2. Have a group of students prepare a picture-answer key for each activity.
3. Place answers on the bottoms of containers for items to be tasted and smelled.
4. Place all answers on an "Answer Tape."

C. Other ways to provide directions for the activity

1. Tape all directions.
2. Illustrate each step of the directions with a series of sketches. (Students could prepare sketches.)
3. Photograph a student completing the steps in each activity. Include photos with directions.
4. Present directions by conducting walk-through demonstrations with small groups of students.

IV. How to Adapt the Basic Center Idea to Other Curriculum Areas

A. Reading/Language Arts: Use the same materials described in the Basic Center Idea, parts 1-5. Have students list as many words as they can which describe each item. A list of synonyms could also be compiled. Use any aspect of the activity as a stimulus for creative writing.

B. Math: Place geometric shapes in a "Mystery Box." Students feel shapes and identify them by name. Numerals can also be used.

C. Social Studies: Select items related to specific units in social studies. For example, build activities around foods, sounds, and everyday objects used in colonial America.

Idea adapted from a center developed by Kitty McGrogan, Carroll County, Maryland.

I. Basic Center Idea

Area: Social Studies

Purpose: To reinforce concepts pertaining to a unit on community helpers.

Objectives: Students will be able to identify community helpers. Students will be able to match community helpers with descriptions of their roles.

Materials: Pictures of community helpers such as fireman, policeman, doctor, nurse, etc.

Set of "Who Am I" riddle cards describing the role of each community helper. For example, "I help to keep children and grown-ups healthy and strong. When people are sick they come to see me. Who Am I?"

Set of "Who Can Help Me" problem cards on which are written statements of problems community members are having. For example, "My garage is on fire. Who Can Help Me?"

Three boxes to contain pictures and cards

Large community map with clearly marked locations such as doctor's office, fire station, etc.

Directions: 1. Take the community helper pictures from the box and look at them carefully.
2. Place each community helper on the community map to show where the helper works.
3. Read the "Who Am I" riddle cards. Match each riddle card with the community helper it describes.
4. Read the "Who Can Help Me" problem cards. Place each card beside the person who can help with the problem.

Evaluation: Self-check: Number coding on the back of the cards corresponds to the number which appears on each commuity helper picture.

II. How to Extend the Basic Center Idea

A. To make the activity easier

1. Limit the number of community helpers to four or five most familiar to students.
2. Have students match pictures of community helpers with pictures showing where the helpers work or with pictures showing the helpers at work.
3. Attach the picture of the community helper to the riddle card. Have students match name cards with the picture-riddle cards.

B. To make the activity more difficult

1. Have students write riddle cards describing what each community helper does.
2. Have small groups of students prepare a mini-telephone directory. List telephone numbers of all the community helpers included in the activity.
3. Have students use several pages from a telephone book or an entire telephone book to solve problems, such as: "Which fire company would you call if a fire occurred?" or, "Which service station is closest for the man who ran out of gas?"

C. To make the activity open-ended

1. Have students create additional problem cards and indicate on a separate answer key which community helper could assist with the problem.

2. Have students write a script for a play describing how a community helper offered assistance to a community member. (Students could produce the play themselves or plan a puppet show.)
3. Have students prepare a community services directory in which each community helper would be pictured along with a description of his or her role, and an address and telephone number appropriate for that locale.

III. How to Modify the Basic Center Idea

A. Other ways to make the center activity manipulative

1. Mount pictures of community helpers on pocket cards. Have students place riddle cards and problem cards in the appropriate pocket cards.
2. Attach pictures of community helpers to center section of a bulletin board. Place riddle cards at random on one side of the pictures and problem cards on the other side of the pictures. Attach two strips of yarn to each community helper picture. Students use yarn strips to match helpers with riddle and problem cards.
3. Prepare a concentration game which includes a set of picture cards and a set of riddle cards.

B. Other ways to provide feedback about the activity

1. Use a separate answer key.
2. Take several snapshots of the completed activity. Students compare their work with the snapshots.

C. Other ways to provide directions for the activity

1. Tape directions.
2. Place each step in the directions on a separate card which includes a sketch of the activity being described.

IV. How to Adapt the Basic Center Idea to Other Curriculum Areas

A. Reading/Language Arts: Match riddle cards describing characters in familiar stories with pictures of those characters.

B. Science: Match riddle cards describing simple machines with pictures of those machines.

C. Math: Match riddle cards describing geometric shapes with the shapes; match problem cards requiring simple computation with cards on which the answer is pictured.

I. Basic Center Idea

Area: Social Studies

Purpose: To introduce a unit on careers

Objectives: Students will describe, compare, and contrast various types of careers. Students will describe the experiences that might help them prepare for various types of careers.

Materials: An envelope for each career to be studied containing the following materials:

> A tape describing the career, preferably taped by a person following that career
>
> Note: The tape might include a description of the career, its advantages and disadvantages, and ways to prepare for it.
>
> Pictures illustrating various aspects of the career
>
> Index cards containing sentences describing the pictures
>
> A set of multiple choice type questions reviewing major aspects of information presented on the tape
>
> Separate answer key.

Directions: 1. Choose one of the envelopes and take the tape, pictures, and index cards from the envelope.
2. Listen to the tape.
3. Match the sentences on the index cards with the pictures. Check your work with the number code on the back of the cards and pictures.
4. Read each question on the paper in the acetate cover and check the appropriate answer. Check your answer with the answer key. Erase your answers from the acetate cover before returning it to the envelope.

Evaluation: Self-check: Number coding and separate answer key.

II. How to Extend the Basic Center Idea

A. To make the activity easier

1. Use the activity for reinforcement after initial presentation as a teacher directed activity.
2. Coordinate the pictures with the taped presentation.
3. Include questions on the tape, following the presentation.

B. To make the activity more difficult

1. Have students prepare the tapes, pictures, and questions as a reinforcement activity after initial presentation as a teacher directed activity.
2. Prepare a set of "career cards" for students to use after studying individual careers. On each card write a statement describing some aspects of a specific career. Include statements for each career previously studied. Students match statements with career.
3. Prepare a set of cards describing the type of activities a person enjoys doing. Have students choose which careers might be best for that person. For example, "Jim enjoys being outdoors, and is quite interested in trees, plants, and wildlife. He goes camping as often as possible. He is active in the Ecology Club in school. What careers might be best suited for Jim?"

C. To make the activity open-ended

1. Have students identify careers which interest them and prepare a learning center activity on that career.
2. Have students interview people in various careers. Students prepare a brief summary of the interview and display it in the center.

III. How to Modify the Basic Center Idea

A. Other ways to make the center activity manipulative
   1. Use pocket cards for question-answer activities.
   2. Use objects that refer to certain careers rather than pictures in the matching activities.
   3. Use puzzle cards for question-answer activities.
B. Other ways to provide feedback about the activity
   1. Include questions and answers on tape.
   2. Use a separate answer key for all activities.
   3. Identify a "center helper" for each career envelope.
C. Other ways to prepare directions for the center
   1. Include directions for each activity on tape.
   2. Present directions for each activity on the front of the envelope containing materials for that activity.

IV. How to Adapt the Basic Center Idea to Other Curriculum Areas

A. Reading/Language Arts: Have students listen to taped stories or newspaper articles. They match pictures about the stories with statements describing the pictures. Finally, students answer questions about the taped stories.
B. Math: Have students listen to taped word problems. After each problem, taped questions are presented to determine if students have identified key information in the problem. (Students do not need to solve the problems.)
C. Science: Have students listen to taped information about designated topics in science. Questions concerning taped material are presented at the end of the tape. Students respond to questions using prepared answer sheets corresponding to the taped questions.

I. Basic Center Idea

Area: Social Studies

Purpose: To introduce a unit on ecology.

Objectives: Students will describe examples of pollution and explain their causes.

Materials: Photos and/or magazine and newspaper pictures illustra-
ting different types of pollution
Folder
Separate answer key
Tape.

Directions: 1. Work in groups of three.

2. Take the pictures from the folder and study them carefully. Then answer the questions below:

   a. What is alike about the pictures?
   b. What caused the problem that you see in each picture?
   c. Group the pictures according to what you think caused the problem.
   d. Find other pictures that could go in each group.
   e. Describe how you would prevent the problems shown in one of your groups of pictures.

Evaluation: Self-check: Number coding or separate answer key according to groupings.

II. How to Extend the Basic Center Idea

A. To make the activity easier

1. Prepare a sentence card to go with each picture stating what caused the pollution problem shown in that picture. Students match pictures with sentence cards.
2. Provide cards on which are listed categories such as, problems caused by man, problems caused by weather, etc. Students group pictures into appropriate categories.

B. To make the activity more difficult

1. Have students work in teams to list examples of pollution in the environment. Provide filmstrips and printed materials for students to use for reference.
2. Have students categorize items from A (see above) according to the cause of the pollution.

C. To make the activity open-ended

1. Have students tour the school area in teams to identify instances of pollution.
2. Have students work in teams to plan what they could do during an "Ecology Week" at school.
3. Have students prepare posters or write television commercials to focus public attention on problems of pollution.
4. Have students create a series of pictures illustrating how an unpolluted area became polluted.

III. How to Modify the Basic Center Idea

A. Other ways to make the center activity manipulative

1. Mount each picture on a pocket card. On the pocket, list possible causes for the pollution problem. Students identify the appropriate cause.
2. Have students use a filmstrip or slide projector to present pictures of polluted areas for study.

B. Other ways to provide feedback about the activity

1. Schedule discussion groups for evaluation purposes.

C. Other ways to prepare directions for the center

    1. Tape directions.

    2. Give directions orally.

    3. Provide several examples for each activity.

IV. How to Adapt the Basic Center Idea to Other Curriculum Areas

A. Reading/Language Arts: Have students compare and contrast sets of pictures and note how they are alike and how they are different. Students group the pictures into categories and then find pictures which fit those categories.

B. Math: Have students study sets of pictures to note common geometric configurations. Students locate pictures with similar geometric configurations.

C. Science: Have students study sets of animal pictures to determine how the animals are alike and how they are different. Students then categorize the pictures, and find other pictures which fit the categories.

I. Basic Center Idea

Area: Social Studies

Purpose: To reinforce a unit on the settlement of the thirteen American colonies.

Objective: Students will describe major events in the settlement of the thirteen American colonies.

Materials: Pockets to contain cards
Sets of cards containing important events in the settlement of the thirteen American colonies
Sets of cards listing persons noted for their involvement in the above events
Time line (yarn or construction paper strip) displayed on a bulletin board
Cards with dates corresponding to the events described
Answer keys.

Directions: 1. Take the cards from pocket 1. On each card is a description of an important event in the settlement of the thirteen colonies. Place the cards along the time line on the bulletin board in the order in which the events occurred. Check your work with the answer key.

2. Take the cards from pocket 2. Names of people appear on these cards. Match the names of the people with the appropriate events on the time line. Check your work with the answer key.

3. Choose one of the events along the time line which you feel is of major importance in the settlement of the thirteen colonies. Write a paragraph describing the event, and why you feel it is important.

Evaluation: Self-check: Separate answer keys for Activities 1 and 2. Teacher evaluation for Activity 3.

II. How to Extend the Basic Center Idea

A. To make the activity easier

1. Limit the number of events to be placed on the time line to a few of major significance.

2. Have students match previously prepared descriptions of the events with the events listed on the cards rather than writing descriptions of those events.

3. Have students match pictures with events rather than person's names with events.

4. Permit students to use their textbooks (or other reference material) as needed to complete the activities.

B. To make the activity more difficult

1. Increase the number of events to be placed on the time line.

2. Have students prepare individual time lines for a specified set of events.

3. Have students categorize the events according to the nature of those events, that is, political, economic, social, or religious.

4. Have students write descriptions of more than one event.

C. To make the activity open-ended

1. Have students select events to place on a time line. Students prepare a set of "event cards" and individual time lines.

2. Have students write a short play about one of the events. The play should emphasize why the event was important in the settlement of the thirteen colonies. Plays can be presented to groups of peers.

3. Have students work together to prepare a script for a T.V. news-cast which would describe an important historical event as if it had just happened. Maps, pictures, or transparencies could be included.

III. How to Modify the Basic Center Idea

A. Other ways to make the center activity manipulative

1. Attach magnetic strips to the back of the event cards and to a time line on a magnetic board.
2. Use a long pocket chart for a time line.
3. Use clothespins to attach cards to a "clothesline" time line.

B. Other ways to provide feedback about the activity

1. Use a number or letter coding system for all matching activities.
2. Let students use information from textbooks to check responses.

C. Other ways to prepare directions for the center

1. Use the activity first as a teacher directed activity with directions explained by the teacher.
2. Directions for each activity could be presented separately rather than being listed together.

IV. How to Adapt the Basic Center Idea to Other Curriculum Areas

A. Reading/Language Arts: Use a "time line" format to have students place in sequence the events from fiction or non-fiction material which they have read.

B. Math: Have students order numerals from smallest to largest along a number line.

C. Science: Have students place in sequential order the steps in an experiment or steps in a chemical or biological process, e.g., photosynthesis.

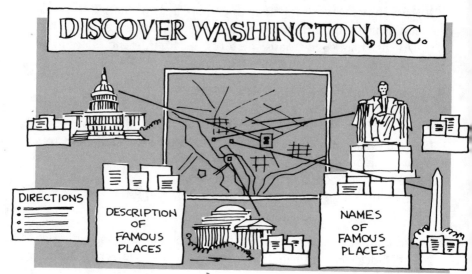

I. Basic Center Idea

Area: Social Studies

Purpose: To reinforce concepts pertaining to a unit on Washington, D.C.

Objectives: Students will identify significant areas in the nation's capital. Students will explain the significance of the areas.

Materials: Cards   Pockets
Envelopes   Pictures.
Map of Washington, D.C.

Directions:
1. Study the map of Washington, D.C.
2. Read the descriptions of famous places in Washington, D.C. that are written on the cards on the bulletin board.
3. Read the names of famous places written on the cards on the bulletin board.
4. Match the name of each place with the description of that place, and put the appropriate cards in the pocket next to the picture.
5. Check your work by matching the number on the back of the cards with the number on the pocket.

Note: The basic center idea is applicable to the study of any city.

Evaluation: Self-check: Numbers on the back of the cards correspond to the number on the pocket.

II. How to Extend the Basic Center Idea

A. To make the activity easier

1. Use pictures on the pockets, and have students match the name of the place with the picture of that place.
2. Limit the written descriptions to very well known places.
3. Have a guide book available for student reference.

B. To make the activity more difficult

1. Include some distractors in the group of cards listing names of places.
2. Include some important, but less well known places in Washington, D.C., such as the Library of Congress.
3. Present descriptions of the places, and have students write the names rather than supplying them on cards.

C. To make the activity open-ended

1. Have students identify places of importance through activities such as these:
   a. You are writing a letter to a friend who is going to Washington, D.C. for the first time. What three places would you tell him are most important to see, and how would you describe these places to him?
   b. You are to take a visitor from another country on a tour of Washington, D.C. You will be taking him to the White House, the House of Congress, and the Lincoln and Jefferson Memorials. What would you explain about each? Practice with a partner, and then record your comments on the cassette tape.
2. Have students react to questions such as these:
   a. How do you think Lincoln would react if he were to visit the Lincoln Memorial for one day?
   b. If you were to design a memorial to one of your heroes from American History, whom would you choose, and what type of memorial would you design?
   c. If a visitor to our country were able to go only to the Smithsonian Institute, do you think he would know much about our country? Why?
3. Have small groups of students make sets of cards with pictures and/or descriptions of famous places in Washington, D.C.

III. How to Modify the Basic Center Idea

A. Other ways to make the center activity manipulative

1. Place cards in a folder or large envelope.
2. Use paper plate and clothespin format.
3. Use a puzzle format.
4. Use a matching activity with yarn or shoestrings.
5. Prepare a concentration game using name cards and description cards.

B. Other ways to provide feedback about the activity

1. Provide a separate answer key.
2. Tape the answers.

C. Other ways to prepare directions for the center

1. Tape the directions.

IV. How to Adapt the Basic Center Idea to Other Curriculum Areas

A. Reading/Language Arts: Prepare matching activities such as the following: match picture, paragraph, or article with title; match word with its antonym, synonym, or homonym; match word with its part of speech.

B. Math: Construct matching activities such as these: match problem with solution; match "word problem" with process used for solution.

C. Science: Design matching activities such as these: match machine with type of simple machine it exemplified; match leaf with name of tree from which it came.

Notes

Notes

Notes

Notes

Chapter 8

Annotated Bibliography

Where can I obtain more information related to learning centers?

Sources Describing Learning Centers

Forte, Imogene, and Joy Mackenzie. Nooks, Crannies, and Corners. Nashville, Tennessee: Incentive Publications, Inc., 1972.

> This reference contains information about learning centers and how teachers might develop and use them. It also contains an extensive appendix illustrating various center ideas and techniques for using them.

Gambrell, Linda B., and Robert M. Wilson. Focusing on the Strengths of Children. Belmont, California: Fearon Publishers, 1973.

> This paperback contains numerous ideas for promoting student self-direction, providing materials for students which are designed to build on their strengths, and organizing the classroom for maximum student involvement.

Glasser, Joyce Fern. The Elementary School Learning Center for Independent Study. West Nyack, New York: Parker Publishing Co., 1971.

> This book presents a different view in that the learning center is a room apart for independent study. Many suggestions are included relating to how to develop such learning centers.

Hall, Mary Ann. "Individualizing Instruction Through Learning Centers," Innovations in Reading, ed. Robert M. Wilson. Position Papers in reading, University of Maryland, 1970.

> Organizational considerations for using centers, the role of supervisors and principals in center development, and the evaluation of center activ-

> ities are considered in the article which stresses that children need both freedom to make choices and the opportunity to assume responsibility by assisting in the planning and evaluation of their learning.

Rapport, Virginia and Mary N.S. Parker, (ed.). <u>Learning Centers: Children on Their Own</u>. Washington, D.C.: ASCD, 1970.

> Included in this collection of articles dealing with individualization of instruction is one entitled, "Children on their own -- centers and stations for learning," an article containing pictures and descriptions of learning centers.

Voight, Ralph Claude. <u>Invitations to Learning, The Learning Center Handbook</u>. Washington, D.C.: Acropolis Books, Ltd., 1971.

> Child growth and development and child individuality are stressed in this handbook of ideas for developing and using learning centers. Suggestions are offered for the implementation of centers in the classroom, examples of specific centers are described, and frequently asked questions about centers are presented with suggested answers.

Williams, Lois E. <u>Independent Learning</u>. Washington, D.C.: American Association of Elementary, Kindergarten, and Nursery Education, 1969.

> Many ideas for independent activities for children are offered, and ways of organizing the classroom to encourage and facilitate use of centers are discussed. The suggestions are especially appropriate for primary grade students.

Sources Presenting Ideas and Activities Appropriate for Use in Learning Centers

Bloomer, Richard. <u>Skill Games to Teach Reading</u>. Dansville, New York: The Instructor Publications, Inc., 1969.*

Cooper, Lee Ann and J. David Cooper. <u>Reading Bulletin Boards</u>. Dansville, New York: The Instructor Publications, Inc., 1971.*

Garrison, Evangeline L. Individualized Reading. Dansville, New York: The Instructor Publications, Inc., 1970.*

Gould, Annabelle and Warren Schollaert. Reading Activities. Dansville, New York: The Instructor Publications, Inc., 1967.*

* These four booklets from Instructor Magazine contain specific ideas which can be used to develop center activities.

Handbook for Learning Centers, (Book I, Book II, Book III, Book IV). Ellicott City, Maryland: Allied Publishing Co., 1973.

This set of four booklets presents center ideas for every curriculum area. Each idea includes a color photograph of the center, along with a description of objectives, materials, directions, and method of evaluation for that center. The booklets present ideas for primary and intermediate grades.

Herr, Selma E. Learning Activities for Reading. Dubuque, Iowa: Wm. C. Brown, Publishers, 1970.

The author has compiled numerous suggestions for independent activities for children to reinforce skills in reading. The activities are categorized according to skill area for easy reference. These suggestions are based upon the philosophy that "activities should be experienced in learning and motivating -- not in testing . . . . " The book contains numerous illustrations. Many of the suggestions could be adapted to a learning center format.

Spice Series. Stevensville, Michigan: Educational Service, Inc.

The Spice Series, published by Educational Service, Inc., includes twelve handbooks which describe ideas, games, and activities that could be used in the development of learning centers.

Spice (Primary Language Arts), 1960
Probe (Science), 1962
Plus (Mathematics), 1964
Spark (Social Studies), 1965
Create (Art), 1966

Action (Physical Activities), 1967
Stage (Dramatics), 1968
Rescue (Remedial Reading), 1969
Anchor (Intermediate Language Arts), 1970
Pride (Black Studies), 1971
Launch (Early Learning), 1972
Flair (Creative Writing), 1972

Wagner, Guy, and Max Hosier. Reading Games. Darien, Connecticut: Teachers Publishing Corporation, 1960.

Both easy games and more challenging games are described in this book which includes introductory information concerning planning and constructing reading games. Many of the ideas presented in the book could be adapted for center activities.

Index

128

Learning Centers : A Guide for Effective Use

Information About ...
Instructo Learning Centers

Instructo, a leading publisher of learning aids for the elementary grades, offers Pre-K through Grade 6 Learning Centers.

Over 60 titles in the following areas:

- Language Arts
- High Interest/Low Level Reading
- Metric
- Mathematics
- Social Studies

INSTRUCTO LEARNING CENTERS . . . .

- Self-instructional
- Self-pacing
- Clear directions for children

- Correlated spirit duplicating activities
- Complete Teaching Guide
- Assembly instructions

For complete information, please write:

Instructo/McGraw-Hill
200 Cedar Hollow Road   Paoli, Pennsylvania 19301

341015